LOG CABIN QUILTS

A Brand New Story

Karen Murphy

Martingale®
& COMPANY

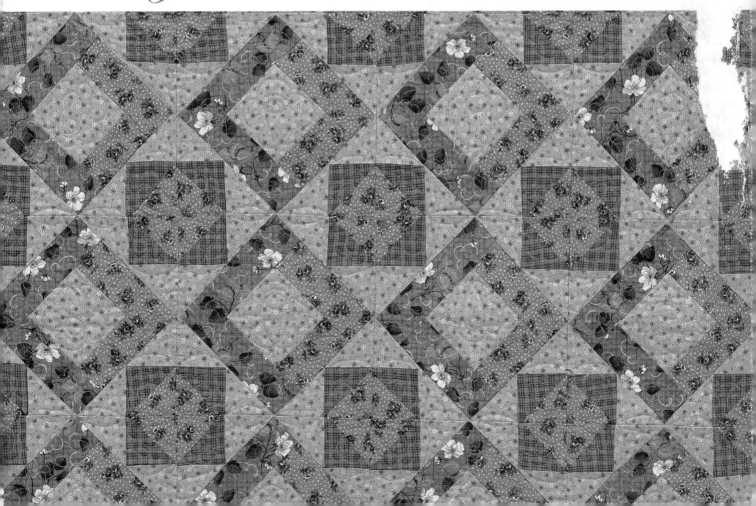

Log Cabin Quilts: A Brand New Story
© 2005 by Karen Murphy

That Patchwork Place® is an imprint of
Martingale & Company®.

Martingale & Company
20205 144th Avenue NE
Woodinville, WA 98072-8478 USA
www.martingale-pub.com

Credits

PRESIDENT: *Nancy J. Martin*
CEO: *Daniel J. Martin*
VP and GENERAL MANAGER: *Tom Wierzbicki*
PUBLISHER: *Jane Hamada*
EDITORIAL DIRECTOR: *Mary V. Green*
MANAGING EDITOR: *Tina Cook*
TECHNICAL EDITOR: *Robin Strobel*
COPY EDITOR: *Melissa Bryan*
DESIGN DIRECTOR: *Stan Green*
TECHNICAL ILLUSTRATOR: *Laurel Strand*
PEN AND INK ILLUSTRATOR: *Kris Lammers*
TEXT DESIGNER: *Trina Stahl*
COVER DESIGNER: *Stan Green*
PHOTOGRAPHER: *Brent Kane*

Mission Statement

*Dedicated to providing quality products and service
to inspire creativity.*

Printed in China
10 09 08 07 06 05   8 7 6 5 4 3 2 1

Library of Congress Cataloging-in-Publication Data
Murphy, Karen.
    Log cabin quilts : a brand new story / Karen Murphy.
        p. cm.
    ISBN 1-56477-588-7
    1. Patchwork—Patterns.   2. Quilting—Patterns.   3. Log
cabin quilts.   I. Title.
    TT835.M8475 2005
    746.46'041—dc22

                                        2004027868

⧼ Dedication ⧽

To my family members, who all believed in me and encouraged me when I thought I didn't have another idea in my head. My children: Shannon and her husband, Josh; Sean and his wife, Shannon; and Brian. My mother, Barbara Williamson, who came over and cleaned my house for me and brought me some delicious meals. My sister, Kris Lammers, who drew the beautiful illustrations and talked through different story ideas with me.

To my friend Karen Bush, who has been my friend through thick and thin, and who gave up several long chatty phone calls because I was working on the book. I owe you lunch!

To my friend Jan Thrasher, who painstakingly helped me with grammar and story ideas. Thank you, Jan, for all the time you spent with me, bringing Abby and George to life.

To all my friends in Mitford who are excited for me and who encouraged me every step of the way.

And thank you to Toni, Jani, Annie, 'Nita, KB, Tonie, Georgia, and Martha, and my fondest remembrances of Pinky and Dorothy. You guys are the best!

Last and most importantly, I give all the credit to my Lord and Savior Jesus Christ, with my heartfelt thank-you for this gift.

 Contents

❧ Prologue ❧

NOTHING WARMS up a room like a quilt. The sight of a quilt instantly evokes memories of childhood, grandparents, or perhaps a snowy day when you were sick with a cold. Quilts speak volumes with just their very existence. It's a nonverbal language that we understand but many times cannot repeat, simply because we don't have the words.

I didn't start out as a quilter. My mother and grandmother taught me to sew when I was in the third grade. That began a love affair with fabric that is still going strong! I made my own clothes and later, when I married, all my children's clothes as well. When my children got old enough to want clothes from the mall, I realized I was tired of making clothes, and I wanted clothes from the mall as well!

I clearly remember the quilt that inspired me to become a quilter. It was a Lone Star wall hanging that had appliqué on the background pieces and was beautifully hand quilted. I never took a quilting class but slowly and laboriously began to teach myself. Of course, I applied garment-making techniques to making quilts! There were so many mistakes, but I learned. And I loved it! The first quilt I made was a Log Cabin wall hanging. Since

then I've made many Log Cabin quilts, from wall hanging to bed size, and sold almost every single one. I still have not gotten around to making a traditional Lone Star quilt, but if you take a look at my quilt "Lone Star Log Cabin" on page 94 you will see my Log Cabin version!

People love Log Cabin quilts. There is a comfort attached to them that seems to defy explanation. In a Log Cabin quilt we see our own history, and the tales of the women who made them, brought right into our own home. No matter if your Log Cabin quilt is made with blues and browns or bright pinks and reds, this quilt style is familiar to almost everyone. It is recognizable and adaptable to nearly any home decor.

As I contemplated Log Cabin quilts and their history, I wondered about the woman who made the first one. What kind of person was she? How did she live her life? Did she have a home in the city or a homestead on the prairie? Bit by bit, the character of Abby introduced herself to me, letting me in on her life and thoughts, and so her story began to take shape. There is much more to Abby than the making of a quilt. She is a woman much like you and me: a wife, a mother, happy, lonely, tired, and eager—we are all made up of conflicting emotions. Perhaps these very conflicts within herself are what led to the creation of the Log Cabin block. One side of the block is generally light and the other side is dark. Contrasting values in fabric make a distinctive pattern, much as our own conflicts give us dimension, warmth, and realism.

Introduction

THE HOT afternoon sun blazed and the air was warm. A grasshopper jumped off a tomato leaf and onto Abby's skirt. She flicked it off with dirty fingers and brushed the stray wisps of hair out of her eyes. The breeze blew slightly. She could hear the distant ring of the ax as her husband and two sons chopped down trees for their first log cabin. Much of the previous year had been spent in a lean-to, drafty and small. They'd had to put off building a cabin; the first priority had been a barn to keep the animals well housed. Milk and eggs were a necessity; without the nourishment they provided, her family could have died. She continued harvesting the turnips and late potatoes. The carrots she would leave to sweeten for another week or so. A good frost would sweeten a carrot nicely.

Life in the wilderness was not easy. Their nearest neighbor was a mile to the south, and the only town was a half day's ride to the west. In the year they had been here, she and her husband, George, had been to town only a few times. Abby met some of the homesteaders' wives there, and they had eagerly visited together. She learned of the quilting bees held monthly and hoped to attend. So far, she had not had the time. The washing, canning, preparing food for drying, weeding the vegetable garden, making the soap, sewing and mending clothing, milking the cow, gathering the eggs, tending to the barn work while the men felled trees for their cabin, and cooking three large meals a day—well, it left very little time for anything else. She had hopes that once the cabin was built, and the men were able to take over the barn chores, she would be free to attend the quilting bees. She longed for the company of other women, their support and their prayers.

Lugging her bushel basket full of potatoes to the root cellar, Abby carefully worked her way down the steps into the darkness of the dug-out room. The shelves were nearly full with corn, beans, and peas. There was no use fooling herself that this work was done; it pretty nearly hadn't even begun. There were the apples, ripening more every day in their little orchard. Some poor soul had tried to tame this land before they arrived and had left a small orchard of apple trees. These would provide some nice dried-apple pies come this winter. Abby shook her head, not even wanting to think about the canning to come. One thing at a time, she told herself.

Now that the wheat harvest was over, George hoped to get the cabin built before butchering began. Abby eyed the large hog in its pen, seeing only bacon and hams for the winter. As she turned back to the vegetable garden, she longed to run inside the lean-to, open her trunk, and find her box of quilt scraps—to feel something in her hands

besides dirt and animals and cast-iron frying pans. A glance at the sun told her there was not enough time to do the things she had to do, let alone something so frivolous. She hurried back to the garden, checking the beans drying on the vine, walking through the spent pea vines to mulch their dried and dead stems back into the earth, and headed for the squash. Much of it was ready to be picked, and with a sigh, she began to search for the best ones, picking as she went.

As she performed this task, her mind wandered. Her back ached and she thought her fingernails would never come clean. The ring of the ax continued in a smooth and even rhythm. Occasionally she would hear a tree crashing through the branches of other trees and landing with a great thump that shook the ground. She always held her breath at that point, waiting to hear the ax again, because that meant her men were all right and nobody had been hurt. The ring of the ax was like a steady melody that lulled her, and under the warmth of the sun she became sleepy.

"Abby!" She spoke to herself sharply, "Get yourself together. Wake up! Quilts! I'll think about the quilting bees." Immediately her mind went back to her box of scraps, most brought from home in Boston, given to her by friends and family. Abby almost hated to use them, especially in a quilt that might be given to someone else. She had to use those pieces in her own quilt. She began to think over the quilt patterns she knew, pausing at each one, wondering if that was the right one for her quilt.

While Abby picked squash and listened to the ax ring out, she glanced at the barn, the logs so perfectly set, chinked with mud to keep it warm for the animals during the long winter. All of a sudden, she had an idea. Abby's mind flashed back and forth from the barn to the picture in her head of her special scraps, and it all came to her in a rush. A square center from the red fabric her dear Aunt Mary had given her would represent the warmth of their hearth. It would be surrounded on all sides by strips of cloth— logs they would be—and on and on her mind raced, everything becoming clear. She would create a special quilt dedicated to the hard work of their first real home on the frontier.

General Instructions

WELL, IT COULD have happened like that! The Log Cabin block has been around since the Civil War days, quickly becoming a popular quilt design. The block was easily made with the scraps left over from sewing dresses, shirts, and bonnets. The pieces required were small strips, and who didn't have those? Pioneer quilters were frugal and used every single bit of cloth and wool. I'm sure they would be astounded if they could see us today—we go to the quilt store, buying fabric specifically for a quilt!

Color arrangement and block placement options opened up a whole new world of design possibilities for the creators of Log Cabin quilts. Quilters could portray the furrows plowed in the prairies. The blocks could be placed to form a diamond of alternating light and dark colors, a setting called Barn Raising. A slight alteration to the

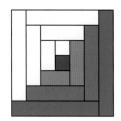

Traditional Log Cabin block

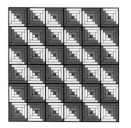

Straight Furrows setting

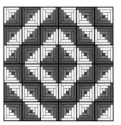

Barn Raising setting

pattern gave us the Courthouse Steps block. The possibilities were endless.

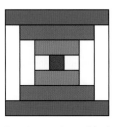

Courthouse Steps block

Traditional Courthouse Steps setting

Log Cabin quilts remain popular today. This book brings the traditional block to a new level with a fresh set of designs that will hang alongside your traditional Log Cabin quilts with pride. I also include a chapter that will help you design parts of your own quilt. The frontier adventure of your Log Cabin quilts is just beginning.

Fabric Selection

I encourage you to buy the best fabric you can afford. Cheap fabric will fade and fray quickly. If you're going to spend a lot of time on your quilt, you want to make sure it will be around for many years to come. The higher-priced fabric is worth it.

Usually two sides of a Log Cabin block are constructed in one colorway with fabrics that are light in value and the other two sides in another colorway with fabrics that are dark in value. High contrast between the two colorways is important to clearly show the design pattern. When you look at the quilts you will see that although I have not always followed the traditional placement of color and value, they are still essential in creating the designs.

Smaller prints, marbled patterns, and solids look great in Log Cabin quilts. These fabrics will have a consistent appearance when cut into small pieces. Large prints may look enticing on the bolt, but when cut into small pieces the value and color often shift dramatically from piece to piece. Choose large prints with care!

I always wash my fabric before using it in a quilt. I've had the awful experience of washing a newly made quilt, only to find one fabric's dye running over the other fabrics. To prewash, put similar colors through a short wash cycle, adding just a little soap and some fabric softener. Dry the fabric on a cotton setting. To restore that "like-new" crispness, spray on fabric sizing (available in any grocery store) while ironing.

Iron your fabric before cutting. Accurate pieces cannot be cut from wrinkled fabric!

Thread

I recommend cotton thread for your machine and the bobbin. Cotton thread has an affinity for cotton fabric, sinking down nicely into the fabric.

Rotary Cutting

My rotary-cutting tools are my best friends in the sewing room! The time they save is incredible. Everyone seems to have an individual method for rotary cutting, and I do, too—I do what seems easiest to me! If you're having trouble getting accurate and easy rotary cuts, try these suggestions.

1. Before cutting, make sure the fabric is folded "on grain." Fold your fabric in half length-wise, starting in the middle and matching the selvage edges. Make sure the fabric hangs straight and has no ripples. If it has ripples, adjust the selvage edges sideways until the fabric is smooth. Don't worry if the cut edges do not match.

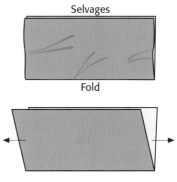

Selvages

Fold

Shift until wrinkles disappear.

2. Align a small ruler along the folded edge of fabric. Place a long 24" ruler on the left side of the smaller ruler, just covering the raw edges of the fabric. Make sure the top edge of the ruler extends above the selvage edges and the long cutting edge of the ruler is just inside one of the cut edges of your fabric.

3. Using your rotary cutter, cut along the edge of the ruler across the width of fabric. Discard the trimmings. Now your edges are straightened and ready to use.

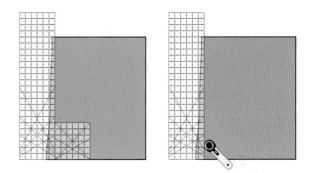

4. Place the long ruler over the straightened edge of fabric so that the correct width of fabric will be cut. Cut the number and size of strips needed.

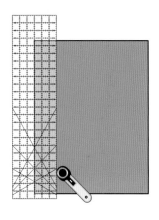

∾

After cutting two or three strips, it is a good idea to straighten your edges again. A slight slipping of the ruler each time you cut can add up to a significantly slanted edge. To straighten the edge, you will again align a horizontal line on the ruler with the folded edge of fabric, and make a cut perpendicular to the fold.

∾

You can use rotary-cutting equipment even when the pattern calls for templates. Permanent templates can be made from plastic sold in most quilt stores, or you can make disposable templates from freezer paper.

1. Using a permanent marker, trace the pattern onto template plastic or the dull side of freezer paper. Include any dots or marks. If you make a permanent template, label the template with the pattern name. (In addition to identifying what the pattern is for, you will always know the right side of the pattern because that will be the side with printing on it!)

2. Using paper scissors or an old rotary blade, cut out the pattern on the outside line. If the pattern consists of all straight lines, I use a ruler and a rotary blade. For curves I like to use scissors.

3. If you are using freezer paper, lightly iron the shiny side of the paper to the right side of the fabric.

4. Place the fabric, right side up, on your cutting mat. You can cut up to six layers of fabric at one time. Be very careful if the pattern is not symmetrical—it must be cut with the right side of the fabric facing up. If the fabric is cut with the wrong side up, the pattern will be cut "reversed" or in a mirror image of what is needed.

5. Place the plastic template, right side up, on the fabric. Place a ruler over the template, aligning the edges. With a sharp blade in your rotary cutter, cut along the edge of the ruler, starting and stopping at the edges of the template. You don't have to use a ruler when cutting; you can cut directly along the edge of the template. However, I find that if I don't cut against a ruler, it is very easy to slice little slivers off the template, making it inaccurate for further use.

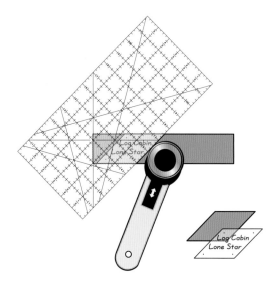

6. Reposition the ruler to cut along the remaining edges of the template.

7. Place the template over the next piece of fabric to be cut. If you use freezer paper, you can peel it off and reuse it several times before it will no longer stick to the fabric and you have to make a new template.

8. If the pattern calls for a shape to be cut "reversed," either place the fabric wrong side up when you cut the shape or place the template with the right side facing down.

Sewing

Sewing accurate quarter-inch seams is important. I recommend using a quarter-inch foot on your sewing machine, but individual variations in machines and sewing habits can still lead to a consistently wide or narrow seam. Check the accuracy of your quarter-inch seams by doing this little test.

1. Cut two strips of fabric 1" x 2". Double-check the widths. You need the pieces to be exactly 1" wide. If your cutting is inaccurate, discard the first two strips and cut two new ones. Precisely cut strips are essential for this test!

2. Place the strips right sides together and sew a seam along one long edge, using your quarter-inch foot. Press the seam to one side. Your finished unit should measure exactly 1½" wide.

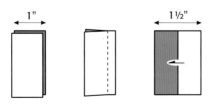

3. If the unit is wider than 1½", your seam allowance was too narrow. Cut, sew, and press two more strips, taking just a tiny bit larger seam allowance. If the sewn unit is narrower than 1½", your seam allowance was too wide. Cut, sew, and press two more strips, this time taking a slightly narrower seam allowance. Make adjustments and keep sewing 1" x 2" strips until you get a finished piece that measures exactly 1½" wide. Now you know how to position the fabric to sew an accurate quarter-inch seam.

At the beginning of a quilt project, I like to cut the pieces for just one block and sew them together before cutting any more fabric. This gives me the opportunity to correct any mistakes before I cut all of my fabric! Once I know I'm making the block correctly, I cut fabric for the remaining blocks (unless specified otherwsie).

Lay the cut pieces out next to your sewing machine and arrange them in the proper block formation. This will ensure that every piece is sewn in the correct order and in the proper place.

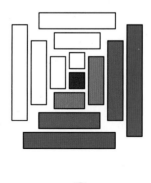

I chain piece everything I can. When you chain piece, the patches for each block are sewn one after the other, without lifting the presser foot. This chain of patches is then cut apart and the seams pressed all at one time.

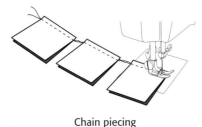

Chain piecing

Log Cabin Construction

Most quilt blocks are made by cutting small pieces of fabric, sewing the pieces together into units, and then combining several units to make the block. Log Cabin blocks are not constructed this way. In Log Cabin construction, two pieces are sewn together and then all the other pieces are added, one at a time, to this unit.

Classic Log Cabin blocks are constructed from the center outward. The first piece is a center square, sometimes called the "hearth," which is then surrounded by "logs"—strips of fabric in various colors.

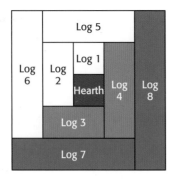

Traditional Log Cabin block

There are many variations to this basic theme. The center hearth can be large or small. Logs can be added to just two sides of the hearth, extra logs can be added to just two sides, or thin logs can be added to two sides and thick logs to the other two

sides—the list can go on and on. If the first two logs are sewn to adjacent sides of the hearth and the remaining logs appear to circle around the center, the construction is usually referred to as "traditional" Log Cabin. If the first two logs are sewn to opposite sides of the hearth, and the third and fourth logs are sewn to the remaining two sides, the block is called Courthouse Steps.

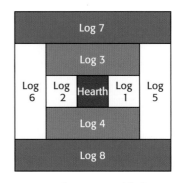

Courthouse Steps block

Traditional Log Cabin Construction

Refer to the following when project instructions direct you to piece according to traditional methods.

1. Sew the first log to one side of the center square. Press the seam toward the log.

2. Hold the unit in front of you, orienting it so the first log is on your right. Turn the unit 90° and sew the second log to the side that is now on your right. I usually rotate my units in a clockwise direction. This results in logs that are added counterclockwise around the center. It is important that you always rotate the units in the same direction so all the blocks in your quilt will match! Press toward the new log.

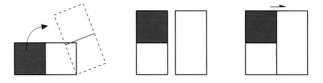

3. Sew the third log to the center unit on the side opposite the first log. Press toward the new log. Sew the fourth log to the unit on the last side of the center square and press toward the log. Your first round of logs is now complete!

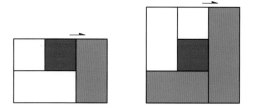

4. You can continue adding as many rounds of logs as you like. The more logs, the bigger the block. Once you have a round of logs sewn, adding another log can get confusing. Which side does it go on? You can tell by examining the ends of the logs. After the first round of logs is complete, always add a new log to the side that has two log ends showing.

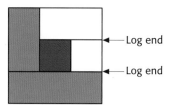

Log Cabin quilt blocks constructed in this manner offer many design possibilities. Traditionally, logs one and two are from the same color family, and logs three and four are from a contrasting color family.

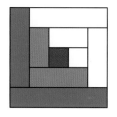

Traditional

It is fun to experiment with nontraditional color placement in your Log Cabin blocks.

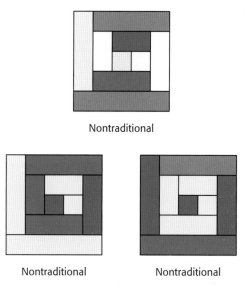

Nontraditional

Nontraditional   Nontraditional

Courthouse Steps Construction

Refer to the following when project instructions direct you to piece according to Courthouse Steps construction.

1. Sew the first two logs to opposite sides of the center square. Press toward the logs.

2. Sew the third and fourth logs to the remaining two sides of the center square. Press toward the logs. Your first round of logs is complete.

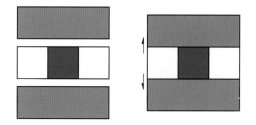

3. Continue to sew logs to the center unit, sewing two logs to opposite sides and then two logs to the remaining sides.

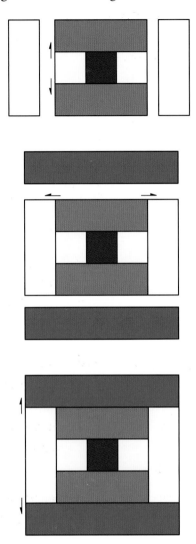

Paper Foundation Piecing

Log Cabin blocks do not have to be square! Start with triangles, diamonds, or hexagons, and add logs to make creative Log Cabin variations. You can make these blocks using traditional piecing methods, but the odd angles make it difficult to sew them accurately. Paper foundation piecing is the answer. Your blocks will be precise and fit together perfectly.

1. Begin by making copies of the pattern. You can do this either by hand or on a copy machine. Make one copy and compare it to the original for accuracy. If your copy machine produces an accurate reproduction, make as many photocopies as the pattern calls for. Only make copies from the original, because the pattern may become distorted if you make copies of a copy. Use a rotary cutter and ruler to trim the excess paper around the pattern. If you are tracing the copies by hand, transfer all interior lines and numbers on the pattern to your copy.

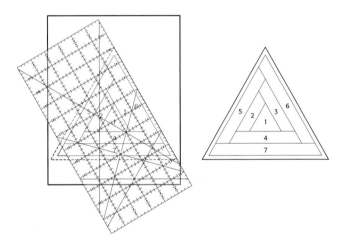

2. Following the project instructions, cut the fabric pieces for each block. The measurements listed for the individual pieces are slightly larger than needed. (I'd rather have too much fabric to cut away than not enough to cover the area.)

3. Shorten the stitch length on your sewing machine. A short stitch will make it easier to remove the papers after the blocks are sewn.

4. The paper-piecing pattern will have numbered segments. Hold the pattern with the numbered side facing you. Place the wrong side of the fabric for piece 1 on the *unprinted* side of the pattern, centering the fabric over the segment 1 area. You can hold the paper up to a light to help position the fabric properly. Make sure the fabric piece not only covers the

entire area but also extends at least ¼" beyond the segment 1 lines. Place the fabric for piece 2 right sides together with piece 1 so that there is approximately a ¼" seam allowance extending into the segment 2 area. If you flip the pattern over, the right side of piece 1 and the wrong side of piece 2 will be facing up. You can pin the pieces to the paper, but if you do, be certain you place the pin so it does not extend into the seam line.

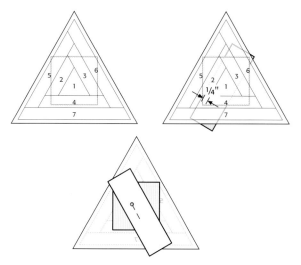

5. Place the pattern with the printed side facing up on your sewing machine. The fabric will be beneath the paper. Start sewing a couple of stitches before the seam line, and then sew directly along the seam line between segments 1 and 2. You will stitch through the paper and fabric layers. Stop stitching a couple of stitches beyond the line. There is no need to backstitch.

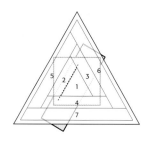

6. With the fabric facing you, fold the paper back and out of the way. Trim the seam to approximately ¼" and press. Sometimes the ink on photocopied paper will transfer onto your ironing board, so use a pressing cloth when ironing.

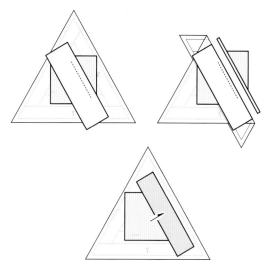

7. Repeating the procedure used in steps 4–6, continue sewing pieces to the block in numerical order until all areas of the pattern are complete. On the outermost pieces, begin and end the seam ¼" beyond the ends of the pattern lines.

8. Trim each block to the edge of the paper (¼" from the outside stitching lines on the pattern).

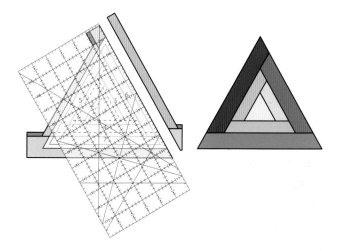

9. Tear the paper off your blocks before piecing them together.

Set-in Seams

Sometimes you will need to join three pieces with a "Y" seam, also known as a "set-in" seam. The technique is the same whether sewing together pieced blocks or single pieces of fabric.

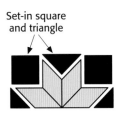

Set-in square
and triangle

1. Place a mark on the wrong side of each patch, ¼" from the corner. You only need to mark the corners that will meet in the "Y" seam.

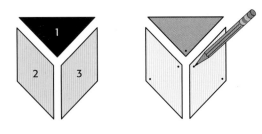

If you are sewing blocks that were made with foundation paper, fold the paper back from the corner and mark the fabric. Tear the paper from the block after the corners are marked.

2. With right sides together and marks matched up, sew patch 1 to patch 2, starting at the edge and stopping and backstitching at the ¼" mark. Only sew to the ¼" mark, not to the edges of the patches! Press toward patch 2.

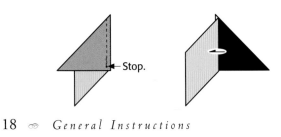

3. With right sides together and marks matched up, align patch 3 with patch 1. Sew from the outside edge to the ¼" mark. Stop and backstitch. Press the seam toward patch 3.

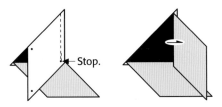

4. Reposition the unit so you can place patch 2 and patch 3 right sides together with their edges matching. Beginning just past the ¼" mark, backstitch to the mark and then stitch the seam to the edge of the patches. Press the seam toward the darker fabric.

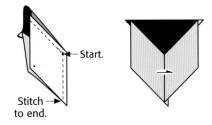

Squaring Up Blocks

No matter how hard we try to piece accurately, it seems we can always end up with one or more wonky, odd-sized blocks. One thing I do with blocks before I sew them together into a quilt top is to "square them." (The exception to this is foundation-pieced blocks, which are already trimmed.) Squaring up blocks can seem tedious, but it's important! Squared-up blocks have a nice even edge and seams that will join neatly during assembly of your quilt top.

Let's say we want the finished block to be 9" square. (By "finished," quilters mean the size of the block once it is sewn into the completed quilt top.) Add the unsewn ¼" seam allowance to each outside edge of the block and you will see that the individual, unfinished block needs to measure 9½".

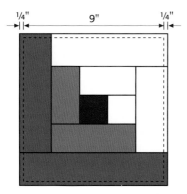

Place the block on a cutting mat and position a large square ruler on top, aligning the lines on the ruler with the block's seams. Measure the block to determine if is too large, too small, or just right. The lines on the ruler will help you see if the block is twisted into a trapezoid or if it has a nice square shape.

If your sewn block is larger than it needs to be, you can square it up by trimming the excess fabric. For example, if your block turned out to be 9¾" square, that's easy: just trim off the extra ¼". Trim two sides and then rotate the block and trim the remaining two sides. Be careful to trim the excess evenly so that the corners form precise 90° angles and the center of the block stays centered.

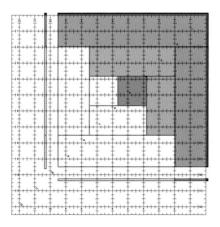

Squaring a block is easy to do if your block is bigger than it needs to be, but what if it's smaller? One of the great things about quilting is the ability to borrow anything you know from any other fiber art and apply it to quilting. We are going to borrow "blocking" from the knitters and apply it to our quilt blocks. After a sleeve or a sweater front is knitted, it can be all twisted out of shape and curled on the edges. Knitters know they need to block the garment to get it to hold the proper shape. We can do the same thing to our quilt blocks if they are too small.

Imagine that your supposed 9½" block measures 9¼" x 9⅜" x 9⅛" x 9⅛". There's nothing to trim! So, we're going to square up the block by blocking it.

1. On a piece of muslin about 12" x 12", draw a 9½" square with a permanent marker. Place this on your ironing board, and grab your pin box. Pin the muslin to your ironing board.

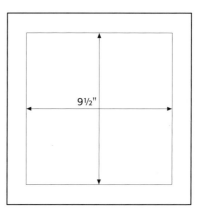

If your block is wider than your ironing board, lay a few towels on a heat-resistant surface. Pin and press on the towels.

2. Lay the quilt block in the center of the muslin square. Spray lightly with water. Delicately pat the block so the outside edges align with the drawn square. At this point, if you're not careful you can stretch your block into all kinds of unsavory shapes. Be very gentle when handling the block. You barely want to touch it with your fingers, patting it into shape.

3. Pin each corner of the block to the muslin, matching the block to the drawn lines.

4. Place another pin at the center of each side close to the edges of the block, again matching the block edges to the lines on the muslin.

5. Carefully pin along the edges of the block, continuing to pat it into shape. You can place as many pins as you like along the block edges.

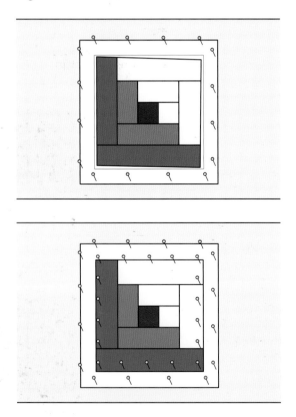

6. When the block edges are aligned with the drawn lines on the muslin, check the block one more time. If there are any puckers, spray the block again lightly with water, and then pat and smooth carefully until the puckers are gone.

7. When you are satisfied with the shape of the block, give it a good mist with water, but don't soak it. Set your iron to a cotton setting and press carefully. "Pressing" is an up-and-down motion with the iron. "Ironing" is a sliding motion. You want to press rather than iron, as ironing can push the block out of shape.

8. Once the block is good and hot, and most of the moisture has steamed away, stop pressing and leave it alone. Let it set, pinned to the ironing board, until completely cool and dry.

9. Unpin and *voilà!* You have a square block measuring 9½".

Using this method, you can be assured that all your blocks will be the same size and your quilt top will be square as well.

Pressing

I like to press all my seams with a steam iron. I think this results in a better-pressed seam than a dry iron. Everyone has his or her own preference. The important thing is that all seams need to be pressed flat, without pleats or distortion.

Borders

Borders need to fit the quilt exactly. Even if directions are followed to a tee, methods of sewing and pressing can alter the size of a quilt's center. I don't give border-length measurements in my cutting instructions because every quilt will be slightly different. You will need to cut your borders to fit your quilt's individual measurements.

There are two different types of borders: those with butted corners and those with mitered corners. Butted borders are the simplest to make.

Borders are sewn to opposite sides of the quilt top, and then the next two borders are added, overlapping the first borders at the corners. (See "Cornerstone" on page 54.) If the quilt has more than one border, the inner borders are completed before the outer borders are added. Mitered borders are a little fancier. All four borders are sewn to the quilt top and then joined at the corners with a diagonal seam. If the quilt has multiple borders, the borders for each side are sewn together before the borders are sewn to the quilt top. (See "Rail Fence Log Cabin" on page 46.)

Butted-Corner Borders

To make borders with perfectly fitting butted corners:

1. Measure the length of the quilt top through the middle to determine the side border lengths. Place a pin at the midpoint of each side of the quilt.

2. Cut your strips to this measurement and place a pin at the midpoint of each strip. Sew the strips to the left and right sides of the quilt top, matching the ends and the pins. If the border is longer than your fabric strips, sew the strips end to end, press, and cut the long strip into border strips the correct measurement. Press toward the borders.

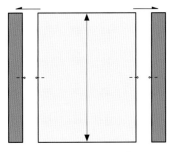

Measure center of
quilt, top to bottom.
Mark centers.

3. Measure the width of the quilt top through the middle, including the side borders just added, to determine the length of the top and bottom borders. Place a pin at the midpoint of the top and the bottom of the quilt.

4. Cut or piece your strips to this measurement and place a pin at the midpoint of each strip. Sew the strips to the top and bottom edges of the quilt, matching the ends and the pins. Press toward the borders.

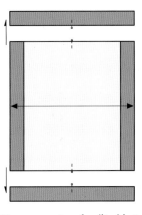

Measure center of quilt, side to
side, including border strips.
Mark centers.

Butted borders

Mitered-Corner Borders

To make borders with mitered corners:

1. Working from the back of the quilt, square up the corners with your ruler and rotary cutter. Make a mark ¼" from each corner.

2. Measure the quilt's width through the center. To this measurement add two times the cut width of the border. Add an additional 2". This will be the length to cut the top and bottom borders. Repeat with the quilt's length to determine the length to cut the side borders. For example, if the center of your quilt measures 48½" x 56", and you plan to add borders that are cut 6" wide, the top and bottom border strips should be cut 62½" (48½" + 6" + 6" + 2" = 62½"). The side border strips should be cut 70" (56" + 6" + 6" + 2" = 70").

3. Mark the center of the border strips and the center point of the sides, top, and bottom of the quilt top. With right sides together and center points matching, pin the borders to the quilt top. The borders will extend past the quilt top at all four corners.

4. Sew the borders to the quilt, stopping and backstitching at the ¼" mark on each corner of the quilt. Be careful not to catch the border from another side in your seam. Press toward the borders.

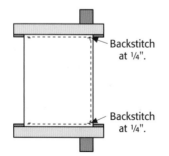

Backstitch
at ¼".

Backstitch
at ¼".

5. Place a corner of the quilt, wrong side up, on a cutting mat. Fold one of the borders out of the way. Align a ruler with the other border, matching a 45° line on the ruler with the border seam and matching the ¼" line to the point where the stitching stops. Cut along the edge of the ruler, being careful to cut only the border!

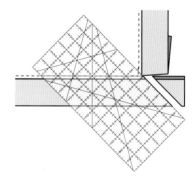

6. Repeat with the corner's other border.

7. Fold the quilt top, right sides together, so the cut edges of the two borders are aligned. Pin. Sew the seam from the inside point to the outer corner, backstitching at the inside point. Press the seam allowance open.

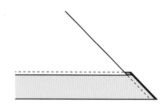

8. Repeat steps 5–7 one corner at a time. Make the cuts, and then immediately sew the seam. To do otherwise will stretch the exposed bias edges. If sewing multiple borders, match the borders at the mitered seam.

Multiple Mitered Borders

If you want multiple mitered borders on your quilt, the border strips for each side of the quilt should be sewn together before you join them to the quilt top. To save on yardage, calculate the length of each border individually. For example, if the center of the quilt measures 48½" x 56" and you want to add an inner 1½"-cut border and an outer 5"-cut border, the inner top and bottom borders should be cut 1½" x 53½" (48½" + 1½" + 1½" + 2" = 53½"). The inner borders will finish at 1", so add twice this measurement to the quilt top to determine how wide the quilt will be once the inner borders are added (48½" + 1" + 1" = 50½"). Calculate the outer top and bottom border measurement using this quilt width (50½" + 5" + 5" + 2" = 62½"). The outer top and bottom borders should be cut 5" x 62½". The side border measurements are determined the same way. The inner side borders should be cut 1½" x 61" (56" + 1½" + 1½" + 2" = 61") and the outer side borders should be cut 5" x 70" (56" + 1" + 1" = 58"; 58" + 5" + 5" + 2" = 70"). Sew the inner and outer borders together for each side, matching centers. These border units will then be sewn to the quilt top.

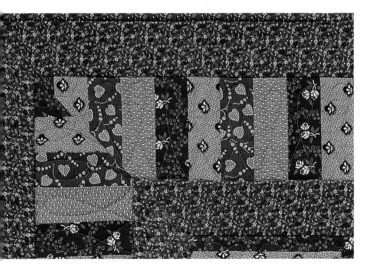

Two borders ready to sew to the quilt top

Three mitered borders

Quilting

Once your quilt top is complete, it needs to be sandwiched to become a finished quilt. The quilt sandwich is composed of three layers: the backing, the batting, and the quilt top. The three layers are joined, usually by either hand or machine quilting.

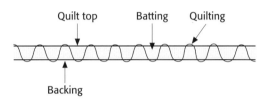

If you decide to have your quilt machine quilted, you can either do it yourself or have a professional quilter do the work. If your quilt is destined to be a family heirloom but you don't have the time to quilt it by hand, you might consider a professional hand quilter. If you have your quilt professionally quilted, check with the quilter to see how much larger than the quilt top you need to make the backing. The batting is often provided by the quilter, so let her know whether you prefer cotton or polyester, and the degree of loft you like. Good communication is essential! Before you leave your quilt with the quilter, talk about the quilting designs, the types and colors of thread, how long the quilting will take, and the estimated cost. Ask to see some of her quilting. Are the stitches relatively even, the curves smooth, and the lines straight? Check the back for knots, loose threads, puckers, and uneven thread tension. I am blessed to have not only one great machine quilter, but two. Ann Trotter and her mother, Mary Decker, are two of the best I've seen.

If you decide to do your quilting yourself, remember that quilting is a skill that improves with practice. Start small, either on a practice piece or on an area of your quilt where the quilting will be least noticeable. Read books, take classes, and ask experienced quilters for their suggestions and help.

Your quilt backing should extend beyond the edges of the quilt top by approximately 5" to 6" on all sides. This applies to both machine and hand quilting. The batting should be the same size as the backing.

Layering

To build your quilt sandwich, find the center of each of the three layers by folding them in quarters. Mark with a pin. Lay out your quilt backing, wrong side facing you, on a large, flat surface such as a table, a bed, or the floor. Some people find it helpful to use masking tape to temporarily attach the edges of the backing to the work surface. Match the center of the batting to the center of the backing, remove the pin from the backing, unfold, and pat smooth. Match the center of the quilt top with the center of the batting, remove the pins and pat smooth. Baste the layers together with safety pins or thread. The basting keeps the three layers from sliding, so how close you place your basting stitches or pins will depend on how slippery your fabrics and batting are. Now your quilt is ready to be quilted.

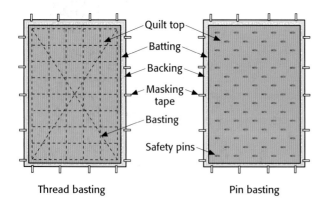

Thread basting   Pin basting

Binding

After the quilting is complete, you will need to finish the edges of the quilt with binding. I use a double-fold binding with mitered corners on all my quilts. The double fold creates two layers of fabric, which provides longer wear on the edges. Mitered corners are easy to make and give a professional look to your quilt. Try them before you decide they are too hard!

1. Measure the length and width of your quilt. Add those numbers and multiply the result by two. You will need this many inches of binding plus 10" to 15" for beginning, ending, and turning the corners. For example, a quilt that measures 48¾" x 57" would need at least 221½" of binding (48¾" + 57" = 105¾"; 105¾" x 2 = 211½"; 211½" + 10" = 221½").

2. Divide the number calculated in step 1 by the usable width of your fabric. (In most cases, this is actually about 40" after the selvages are removed.) Round up the result to the next whole number. This is the number of strips you need to cut. If we continue with the example in step 1, you would need to cut six strips for the binding (221½" ÷ 40" = 5.537). There will be a little bit of unused binding, but it's better to have leftover fabric than not enough to bind the quilt!

3. Sew the short ends of the strips together with a 45° seam to make one long strip. I prefer the 45° seam to a straight seam because it makes a less bulky binding. Press the seam open.

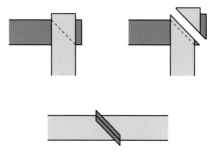

4. Trim one end of your binding at a 45° angle. Turn the end under ¼" and press. This end will be the beginning of your binding. Press the long binding strip in half lengthwise, wrong sides together.

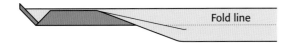
Fold line

5. If you have not trimmed the excess batting and backing from the quilt, do so now. Square each corner of your quilt and make a mark on the right side of the quilt top ¼" from each corner. If the borders are only lightly quilted, it is usually a good idea to baste the edges of the quilt to keep the layers from shifting when you sew the binding. To baste the edges, set your machine for a longer stitch than usual, and run a line of machine stitching ⅛" inside the edge of your quilt top. A walking or even-feed foot will help keep the layers from shifting.

6. Beginning in the middle of one side, align the cut edges of the binding with the edge of the quilt top. Leave the first 3" to 4" of the binding free, and begin sewing the binding to the quilt. When you reach the ¼" mark at the corner, stop sewing and backstitch.

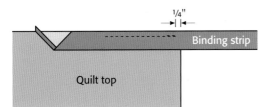
¼"
Binding strip
Quilt top

7. Remove the quilt from the sewing machine and clip the threads. Rotate the quilt 90° counterclockwise. Pull the binding straight up, perpendicular to the side you just sewed, and then bring it down to lie even with the next quilt edge, creating a little triangular fold. Start stitching at the edge of the quilt

and sew to the ¼" mark at the next corner. Backstitch and repeat for each corner.

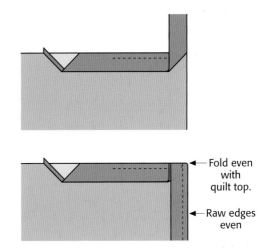
Fold even with quilt top.
Raw edges even

8. Stop sewing about 5" to 6" before you reach the beginning of the binding. Remove the quilt from the sewing machine. Lay the end of the binding over the beginning edge. Allow about ½" to 1" of overlap and cut the end of the binding strip at a 45° angle to match the binding already sewn. Be careful to trim this angle in the same direction as the angle at the beginning of the binding! Tuck the end of the binding into the beginning of the strip. Finish sewing the binding to the quilt.

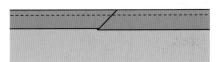

9. Fold the binding to the back of the quilt so that it covers the machine stitching, and hand stitch it in place. Take a couple of tiny stitches in each corner to hold the miter in place and also at the folded edge at the beginning of the binding strip.

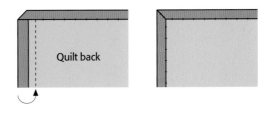
Quilt back

Chapter 1

ABBY'S EYES opened before dawn. She lay snuggled under the quilts, feeling the warmth of her husband next to her. Today was the day. She hugged herself in delight, smothering a giggle. Today, their home would be built. George and their two sons, Sam and Henry, had worked hard to fell the trees and strip the branches. They had spent days hauling rock from the river and constructing the foundation and chimney. Before long their neighbors would arrive to help with the building. "Many hands make light work" was the motto for the day.

Quietly she crept from the bed, her bare feet padding across the cold dirt floor. Soon there would be smooth wood planks under her feet. She opened the stove door and laid bits of kindling on the coals, then shut the door and turned the latch. She set the coffee pot on the back of the stove. The smell of coffee would soon fill the air.

The birds began to twitter, the darkness lifted, and the day had begun. Breakfast was eaten hastily and the men were out the door. Soon she heard the clang of wagon harnesses and the greetings of "Hello" from men as they pulled up.

Abby set up a table in the yard, planks over sawhorses. The women who arrived with their husbands set out their covered dishes. The children ran and played. Abby and the other women sat and stitched on

their quilt pieces, sharing news and gossip. Abby kept her pieces for the Log Cabin quilt, as she had come to call it, in her trunk, not wanting to share her idea just yet. She sat stitching an economical nine patch, made from all her scraps.

"Abby, you have a lovely stitch. Every one is so tiny and even." Mary, her closest neighbor, leaned over to watch.

Abby blushed. "Thank you. I guess I've had a lot of practice. When we lived in Boston, I made a lot of quilts. Where did you move from?"

"Oh, we came from New York," Mary said. "My husband, Franklin, he's wanted to come west for the longest time. We finally saved enough money to buy supplies and make the trip. To tell you the truth, I was glad to leave New York. I know lots of women just have to follow their men wherever they have a hankerin' to go, but I was eager to go." She smiled.

"I wasn't so happy about leaving Boston and all my family. But, I followed!" Abby gave an answering smile. "I'm happy to be here now, although I do miss them."

When the sun rose high in the sky, the women put their quilting away and prepared the meal. The men were hot and thirsty, sweaty and tired. But they all had smiles on their faces. As much as they wouldn't admit it, they enjoyed the company of other men, too. They drank gallons of cold buttermilk

and hot coffee. Crocks of baked beans, platters of roasted pork and turkey, plates of fried chicken, boiled potatoes covered with vinegar, all manner of vegetables, freshly churned butter, and newly baked bread covered the makeshift table. In the lean-to were several chocolate cakes, puddings, and pies of all kinds. They were saved for the afternoon.

Stomachs full, the men returned to work and the women began mixing mud with straw for chinking. Once the heavy logs were raised to the roof and secured, the women began to stuff the cracks between the logs with the mud mixture. It was dirty work.

Abby found herself working next to Mary again.

"From what I can tell, we seem to be the closest neighbors. I hope we get to see more of you . . . and Franklin," Abby quickly amended. "Have you built a cabin yet?"

Mary blew a wisp of hair from her face. "No, we haven't, not yet. Franklin's been collecting logs, but he works alone. Our sons are too young to help; they are only five and six years old. They sure keep me running though!" She laughed.

"Well, maybe your cabin will be the next one we work on." Abby smiled encouragingly, as she rubbed her nose with the back of her hand. "Oh, I hate muddy hands!"

Finally, the chinking was complete, the last shingle was nailed in place, the last window was cut out of the logs—and it was done.

Abby stood next to George and took in the sight of her new home. "It's beautiful!"

He looked down at her, dirt and sweat clinging to his face, and grinned. "You don't expect me to carry you over, do you?"

"Well . . . ," she smiled coyly.

✑ One Room Only ✑

Designed by Karen Murphy, 52" x 62½"
Made by Carol Holmes; quilted by Mary Decker

*L*ike a one-room log cabin, the blocks in this quilt have just one round of logs around
the center square. I've simplified the piecing so you can make the top in
about the time it took to raise the logs around Abby's new home.

A simple block made in two different colors is used to create the quilt.
It could be constructed in the Log Cabin style, but by using Courthouse
Steps and changing the way the logs are sewn to the hearth piece, I've
simplified it even more.

BLOCK NAME: Simple Courthouse Steps
FINISHED BLOCK SIZE: 7½" x 7½"
SKILL LEVEL: Easy

Red block

Blue block

Materials

Yardages are based on 42"-wide fabric.
- 2¼ yards of dark brown print for side and corner triangles, border, and binding
- 1¼ yards of red print for blocks
- ⅞ yard of blue print for blocks
- 3¾ yards of backing
- 62" x 72" piece of batting (twin)

Cutting

Fabric	First Cut
Red	13 strips, 3" x 42"
Blue	9 strips, 3" x 42"
Dark brown	4 squares, 11⅞" x 11⅞"
	2 squares, 6¼" x 6¼"
	6 strips, 5" x 42"
	6 strips, 2½" x 42"

Second Cut

From 8 of the strips, cut 40 rectangles, 3" x 8".
From 5 of the strips, cut 24 rectangles, 3" x 8".
Cut each square twice diagonally to make 16 side triangles. ⊠
Cut each square once diagonally to make 4 corner triangles. ◻

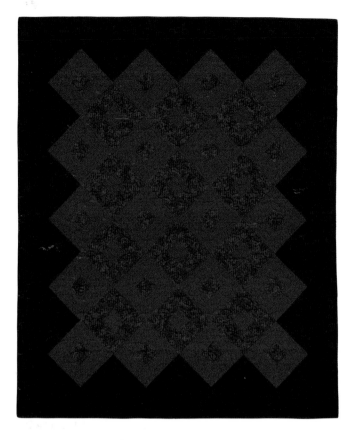

2. From the strip sets, cut 20 segments, 3" wide.

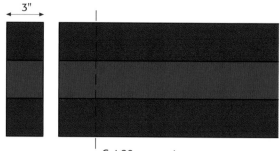

Cut 20 segments.

3. Sew 3" x 8" red rectangles to opposite sides of a unit cut in step 2. Press toward the red rectangles. Repeat to make 20 red blocks.

Make 20.

Block Construction

Blocks are made using modified Courthouse Steps piecing. (See "Courthouse Steps Construction" on page 15.)

Red Block

1. Sew a 3" x 42" red strip to each long edge of one 3" x 42" blue strip. Press toward the red strips. Repeat to make a total of two strip sets.

Make 2 strip sets.

Blue Block

1. Sew a 3" x 42" blue strip to each long edge of the remaining 3" x 42" red strip. Press toward the blue strips.

Make 1 strip set.

2. From the strip set, cut 12 segments, 3" wide.

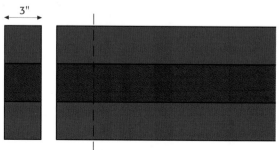

Cut 12 segments.

3. Sew 3" x 8" blue rectangles to opposite sides of a unit cut in step 2. Press toward the blue rectangles. Repeat to make 12 blue blocks.

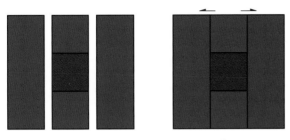

Make 12.

Quilt Assembly

1. Arrange the blocks and the 11⅞" brown side triangles according to the diagram below and the photo on page 30. You will have two unused brown triangles.

2. Place a 6¼" brown triangle at each corner.

3. Sew the blocks and triangles into rows. Press blocks in the opposite direction from row to row. Sew the rows together. Press.

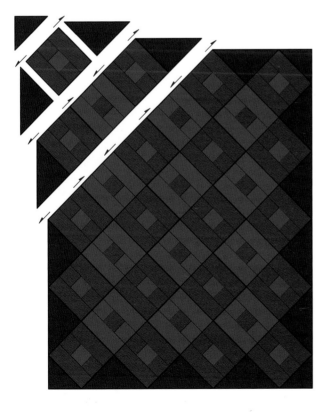

4. Measure the center of the quilt from top to bottom to determine the side border measurements. Piece and cut two borders from the 5" x 42" brown strips to this measurement and sew them to the left and right sides of the quilt top. (See "Butted-Corner Borders" on page 21.) Press toward the borders.

5. Measure the center of the quilt from left to right to determine the top and bottom border measurements. Piece and cut two borders from the 5" x 42" brown strips to this measurement and sew them to the top and bottom of the quilt top. Press toward the borders.

Finishing

1. Your quilt top is complete, and it's time to sandwich it with backing and batting. (Refer to "Layering" on page 24.) Quilt either by machine or by hand. My quilt was machine quilted with an allover flower-and-leaf design. Trim excess batting and backing from the edges.

2. Piece the 2½"-wide brown strips end to end to make one long binding strip. Fold the strip in half lengthwise, wrong sides together, and press. Sew the raw edges of the binding to the front of your quilt. Fold the binding over to the back and hand stitch. (See "Binding" on page 24.)

∞ One Room with a Window ∞

Made by Karen Murphy, 63" x 84¼"; quilted by Mary Decker

bby's cabin had the luxury of windows, which must have brightened her world considerably. In this quilt I used the same block as the previous pattern but brightened the design by adding "windows" in another color. Don't let the design intimidate you—this quilt is very easy to make. The Courthouse Steps block is made in three different color combinations that are then arranged to give the quilt a whole new look.

BLOCK NAME: Courthouse Steps
FINISHED BLOCK SIZE: 7½" x 7½"
SKILL LEVEL: Easy

Block A   Block B

Block C

Materials

Yardages are based on 42"-wide fabric.

- ✧ 2½ yards of red print for blocks and inner border
- ✧ 1½ yards of dark brown print for outer border and binding
- ✧ 1⅜ yards of cream print for blocks and side and corner triangles
- ✧ 1⅛ yards of blue print for blocks
- ✧ 5½ yards of backing
- ✧ 72" x 92" piece of batting (twin)

Cutting

Fabric	First Cut	Second Cut
Red	24 strips, 3" x 42"	From 14 of the strips, cut 70 rectangles, 3" x 8".
	7 strips, 1½" x 42"	
Blue	12 strips, 3" x 42"	From 10 of the strips, cut 48 rectangles, 3" x 8".
Cream	6 strips, 3" x 42"	
	5 squares, 11⅞" x 11⅞"	Cut each square twice diagonally to make 20 side triangles. ⊠
	2 squares, 6¼" x 6¼"	Cut each square once diagonally to make 4 corner triangles. ◺
Dark brown	7 strips, 4" x 42"	
	8 strips, 2½ " x 42"	

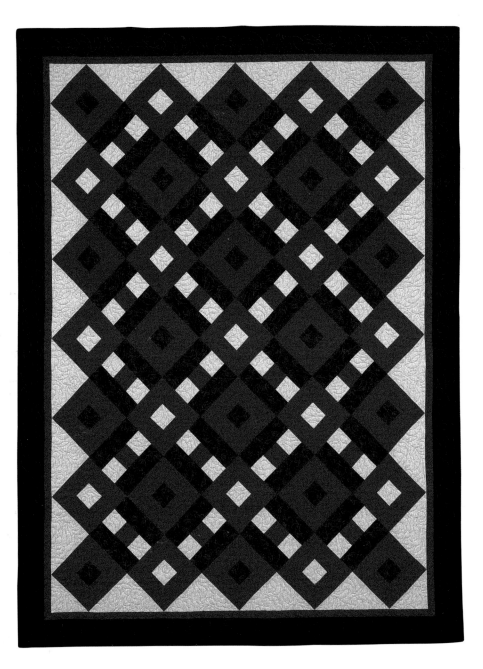

Block Construction

Blocks are made using modified Courthouse Steps piecing. (See "Courthouse Steps Construction" on page 15.)

Block A

1. Sew a 3" x 42" red strip to each long edge of one 3" x 42" blue strip. Press toward the red strips. Repeat to make a total of two strip sets.

Make 2 strip sets.

2. From the strip sets, cut 18 segments, 3" wide.

Cut 18 segments.

3. Sew 3" x 8" red rectangles to opposite sides of a unit cut in step 2. Press toward the red rectangles. Repeat to make 18 of block A.

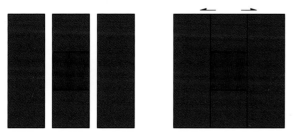

Make 18.

Block B

1. Sew a 3" x 42" red strip to each long edge of one 3" x 42" cream strip. Press toward the red strips. Repeat to make a total of two strip sets.

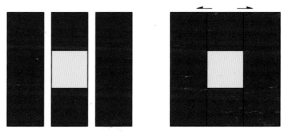

Make 2 strip sets.

2. From the strip sets, cut 17 segments, 3" wide.

Cut 17 segments.

3. Sew 3" x 8" red rectangles to opposite sides of a unit cut in step 2. Press toward the red rectangles. Repeat to make 17 of block B.

Make 17.

Block C

1. Sew a 3" x 42" cream strip to each long edge of one 3" x 42" red strip. Press toward the red strip. Repeat to make a total of two strip sets.

Make 2 strip sets.

2. From the strip sets, cut 24 segments, 3" wide.

Cut 24 segments.

3. Sew 3" x 8" blue rectangles to opposite sides of a unit cut in step 2. Press toward the blue rectangles. Repeat to make 24 of block C.

Make 24.

Quilt Assembly

1. Arrange the blocks and the 11⅞" cream side triangles according to the diagram above right and the photo on page 34. Be sure to turn all C blocks in the proper direction to form the pattern.

2. Place a 6¼" cream triangle at each corner.

3. Sew the blocks and triangles into rows. Press seams in the opposite direction from row to row. Sew the rows together. Press.

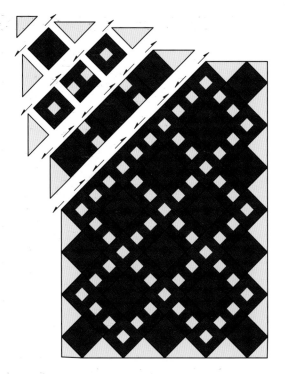

4. Measure the center of the quilt from top to bottom to determine the side border measurements. Piece and cut two borders from the 1½" x 42" red strips to this measurement and sew them to the left and right sides of the quilt top. (See "Butted-Corner Borders" on page 21.) Press toward the borders.

5. Measure the center of the quilt from left to right to determine the top and bottom border measurements. Piece and cut two borders from the 1½" x 42" red strips to this measurement and sew them to the top and bottom of the quilt top. Press toward the borders.

6. Repeat steps 4 and 5 to make outer borders from the 4" x 42" brown strips. Press toward the brown borders.

Finishing

1. Your quilt top is complete, and it's time to sandwich it with backing and batting. (Refer to "Layering" on page 24.) Quilt either by machine or by hand. I chose an allover flower motif for my quilt. Trim excess batting and backing from the edges.

2. Piece the 2½"-wide brown strips end to end to make one long binding strip. Fold the strip in half lengthwise, wrong sides together, and press. Sew the raw edges of the binding to the front of your quilt. Fold the binding over to the back and hand stitch. (See "Binding" on page 24.)

Chapter 2

GEORGE PUT the finishing touches on the cabin. Real glass windows were set into oak frames. No oiled paper windows in this home! During the winter, he and the boys had crafted a solid oak door that now hung with forged metal hinges. Their home would not only be cozy, but solid.

In the lean-to, Abby folded sheets and quilts and placed them in baskets. The kitchen things sat waiting on the table. She looked around, checking for forgotten items.

"Abby, are you ready?" George called from the door.

Abby jumped, her hand on her heart. "George! You scared me!"

He grinned. "I thought you were workin' hard, and here I find you daydreaming!"

"Oh, I was just thinking about our real windows, George. They are so beautiful!" She smiled into his eyes. "Thank you for our new home."

His face grew red. "Well, it's nothin'. The least I could do after dragging you out here into the wilderness with me. Come on, let's get these things in the house." George grabbed a stack of pots and pans and headed out the door. Abby picked up her basket of quilts and followed.

Sam and Henry helped bring over the bed. After it was set up, Henry cleared his throat.

"Um, well, me an' Sam, we were thinkin', I mean, we think we'll just stay in the lean-to. For sleepin' that is; we'll come over to eat an' all."

Abby looked up from tucking in a sheet. "Stay in the lean-to? Whatever for? We have this lovely new home with a wood floor and real windows . . . " Her voice trailed off as she looked at them quizzically.

"Well, I . . . uh, I mean we . . . well, we just want to." Henry looked at his father for help.

"Yeah, go ahead," George said.

Abby crinkled her forehead. "George? I don't understand."

He came over and patted her shoulder. "I know, but it's all right." And he headed over to the lean-to for another load.

Abby stared after him in disbelief. She sighed, shook her head and went about putting her pots away on the shelves built into the wall.

That night, after supper had been served in their new home, the two boys rose and said good night.

Abby started toward them to give them a kiss, but they backed away. Their faces were red, and they stumbled over their feet as they left.

Eyes filling with tears, she said, "I don't understand. I thought we'd all be together."

"Sweetheart, they are nearly grown men. It's natural for them to become more

independent. I've seen Henry eyeing the Lewis girl—what's her name? Uh, Rebecca! Soon they'll be getting married. I also think they want to give us privacy." He raised one eyebrow and grinned rakishly.

This time it was Abby who blushed furiously. "George!"

"You wanted to know!" His grin seemed permanently affixed to his face. "I'm going out to the barn. I'll be back soon."

Abby poured hot water into her dishpan and washed the dishes. The more she thought about it, the more she realized how nice it would be for them to be alone. It had been a few years since they'd had their own room. And now that George mentioned it, she had noticed Henry and Rebecca spending time together. Henry, getting married! Why, she could be a grandmother soon! The thought hit her like cold water and she gasped. A grandmother! She barely felt old enough to be their mother! But the thought of a baby thrilled her and she smiled. She and George had always wanted more children, but God had blessed them with two and no more. A grandmother!

Maybe she'd better start working on a few small quilts and perhaps some warm buntings. Her mind raced with thoughts of grandmothering. She hurried through the dishes, anxious to search her trunk for suitable material.

George stomped his feet free of dirt on the porch and came inside.

"George! Do you realize we could be grandparents soon?" She beamed. "Just think, a new baby!"

He blanched and stared at her. "Grandparents?" His voice broke.

"Yes, you know, if Henry marries Rebecca, naturally they'll have children. That would make us grandparents," she explained slowly.

George blinked and sat down. "Grandparents?" He finally focused on her, his mouth slightly ajar.

"Yes, Grandpa," she teased. "And close your mouth; it makes you look simple."

He shook his head. "I don't feel like a grandpa." Winking at her, he added, "And you don't look like a grandma!"

❧ A Crooked Path ❧

Made by Karen Murphy, 70" x 85"; quilted by Mary Decker

As Abby and George settle into their new home, they realize their future may hold a few surprises. After all, life seems to travel more frequently on a crooked path than on a straight one! This quilt has a few surprises as well. What happens when you make the center of a Log Cabin block the brightest part of the design? What if you combine it with a similar block, but one with a different-sized center? Fun, that's what happens! Each block has just one round of logs, making this project quick and easy.

BLOCK NAME: Courthouse Steps
FINISHED BLOCK SIZE: 10" x 10"
SKILL LEVEL: Easy

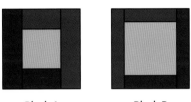

Block A   Block B

Materials

Yardages are based on 42"-wide fabric.
- 2¼ yards of green print for blocks
- 2¼ yards of brown print for blocks
- 2¼ yards of plaid for side and corner triangles and binding
- 1⅞ yards of gold print for blocks
- 5½ yards of backing
- 82" x 96" piece of batting (double)

Cutting

Fabric	First Cut	Second Cut
Green	12 to 14 strips*, 3" x 42"	From 8 (or 10)* of the strips, cut 30 rectangles, 3" x 10½".
	1 strip, 3" x 21"	
	9 to 11 strips*, 2⅛" x 42"	From 5 (or 7)* of the strips, cut 20 rectangles, 2⅛" x 10½".
Gold	4 strips, 5½" x 42"	
	1 strip, 5½" x 21"	
	4 strips, 7¼" x 42"	
Brown	12 to 14 strips*, 3" x 42"	From 8 (or 10)* of the strips, cut 30 rectangles, 3" x 10½".
	1 strip, 3" x 21"	
	9 to 11 strips*, 2⅛" x 42"	From 5 (or 7)* of the strips, cut 20 rectangles, 2⅛" x 10½".
Plaid	5 squares, 15½" x 15½"	Cut each square twice diagonally to make 20 side triangles. ⊠
	2 squares, 8" x 8"	Cut each square once diagonally to make 4 corner triangles. ◲
	9 strips, 2½" x 42"	

*The number of strips you need to cut will depend on the usable width of your fabric. By the time you cut off the selvages, many fabrics are closer to 40" wide than 42" wide, and that can make quite a difference! Start by cutting the smaller number of strips. If you can't cut enough pieces from those strips, you will have to cut more strips. For example, from the green 3" x 42" strips, if you can cut four 10½"-long rectangles from each strip, you need only 8 strips for the rectangles (12 strips total). If you can cut only three 10½"-long rectangles from each strip, you will need 10 strips for the rectangles (14 strips total).

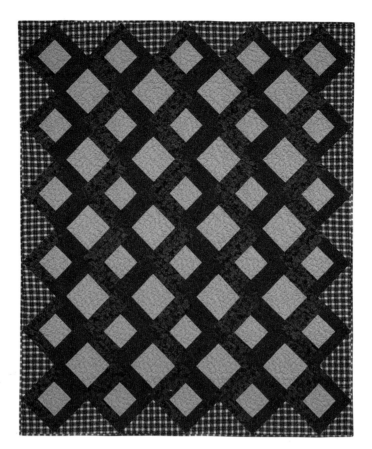

Block Construction

Blocks are made using modified Courthouse Steps piecing. (See "Courthouse Steps Construction" on page 15.)

Block A

1. Sew a 3" x 42" green strip to one long edge of a 5½" x 42" gold strip. Sew a 3" x 42" brown strip to the other long edge of the gold strip. Press away from the gold strip. Repeat to make a total of four strip sets. Make an additional half-length strip set, using the 5½" x 21" gold strip, the 3" x 21" green strip, and the 3" x 21" brown strip.

Make 4½ strip sets.

2. From the strip sets, cut 30 segments, 5½" wide.

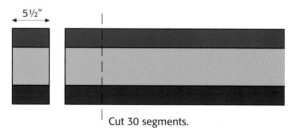

Cut 30 segments.

3. Sew a 3" x 10½" green rectangle to one side of a unit cut in step 2. Sew a 3" x 10½" brown rectangle to the other side. Press toward the rectangles. Repeat to make 30 of block A.

Block A.
Make 30.

Block B

1. Sew a 2⅛" x 42" green strip to one long edge of a 7¼" x 42" gold strip. Sew a 2⅛" x 42" brown strip to the other long edge of the gold strip. Press away from the gold strip. Make four strip sets.

Make 4 strip sets.

2. From the strip sets, cut 20 segments, 7¼" wide.

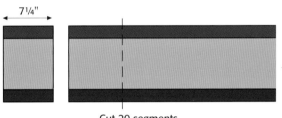

7¼"

Cut 20 segments.

3. Sew a 2⅛" x 10½" green rectangle to one side of a unit cut in step 2. Sew a 2⅛" x 10½" brown rectangle to the other side. Press toward the rectangles. Repeat to make 20 of block B.

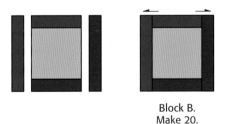

Block B.
Make 20.

Quilt Assembly

1. Alternating A blocks and B blocks, arrange the blocks according to the diagram above right and the photo on page 42. Be careful to rotate the blocks so that the brown logs in the A blocks are next to the brown logs in the B blocks, and the green logs in the A blocks match up with the green logs in the B blocks.

2. Add the 15½" plaid side triangles and the 8" plaid corner triangles to the block layout. You will have two side triangles left over.

3. Sew the blocks and triangles into rows. Press in the opposite direction from row to row. Sew the rows together. Press.

Finishing

1. Your quilt top is complete, and it's time to sandwich it with backing and batting. (Refer to "Layering" on page 24.) Quilt either by machine or by hand. My quilt is machine quilted with an allover oak leaf design, echoing the oak leaves found in my fabric. Trim excess batting and backing from the edges.

2. Piece the 2½"-wide plaid strips end to end to make one long binding strip. Fold the strip in half lengthwise, wrong sides together, and press. Sew the raw edges of the binding to the front of your quilt. Fold the binding over to the back and hand stitch. (See "Binding" on page 24.)

Chapter 3

ABBY SET her yellow bowl filled with rising bread dough on her kitchen worktable by the stove. She covered it with a towel and checked the venison roast in the oven. The roast filled the room with savory aromas and started her stomach growling with hunger. She poured herself a cup of coffee and placed two cinnamon raisin cookies on a plate.

Abby sat at the table, sipping coffee and thinking over the last week. The weather had finally turned cold enough to butcher. Hams were hanging in the smokehouse. Bacon was salted down in its own barrel. She finished the week making enough soap to last the winter.

Now that the cabin was finished, the men took over the barn chores and Abby was finally left to her home. She could wear

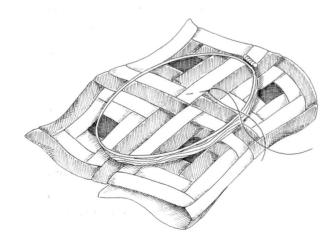

a nicer dress and begin to feel like a woman again, rather than a plow horse that simply worked from dawn till dusk. A few times, when George and the boys were hunting, she had worn her husband's britches to do the barn work. She laughed out loud as she pictured the look on George's face had he come home to a wife in britches!

The garden work was done. In the root cellar, the shelves were groaning with jars of vegetables and the floor was covered with barrels of apples, carrots, and potatoes.

The glass windows sparkled in the afternoon sun and threw sunbeams over the room. It was still hours before supper, so Abby took out her Log Cabin quilt pieces and began cutting some strips from the dark blue she had used on George's shirt. There was also the brown she had used on Samuel's shirts and the darker brown from Henry's. The red centers were already cut.

In her sewing basket, the extra white cotton from a petticoat spilled over the edge. What if half of the block was made of dark logs and the other half of light logs? Quickly she cut some strips from the white and laid them on the table next to a red center. Oh it was beautiful, she thought to herself. The blocks would form diagonal rows of color when they were sewn together. She had never seen a quilt like this and was more eager than ever to start. She wondered how many rows of logs there should be. She

rearranged the strips on the table. First five rows of logs, then seven. Maybe that was too many. She took away a row of strips. Six rows looked just about right.

Quite content with her plan, she sat in her rocking chair and stitched the afternoon away. Her thoughts meandered around her son's upcoming wedding and the baby sure to follow. Some of Aunt Mary's red fabric was waiting to be made into a baby quilt.

Henry was gone many evenings a week now, courting Rebecca. That girl was a bit high-spirited for Abby, who had long envisioned a sweet, submissive companion for her gentle son. Rebecca's saving grace was that she was strong and sturdy. She'd be able to help Henry with all the work that starting a new home and farm entailed. As a wedding gift, Abby and George were giving a section of their land to the young couple. In order to have a home ready for his bride, Henry was already out felling trees from that area. Abby was thrilled to have her son and, hopefully, their new grandbaby so close to home. She would try to like Rebecca, for Henry's sake.

Her thoughts continued on to a new way of setting her garden, and then leaped ahead to the last trip to town before winter set in. They planned to go next week for winter supplies—flour, sugar, coffee, and thread. The most exciting part was the quilting bee, the first one she'd been able to attend. From talking to the ladies at the cabin raising, she knew that they would share lunch and work on the quilt of a newly engaged girl who lived in town. Marriages typically took place in fall, after the harvest was in. Couples had a nice long winter to become better acquainted and settle into their married life. Spring brought plowing and planting, the busiest time of year, and summer saw the welcome arrival of new babies.

Abby's fingers flew and soon she had a stack of blocks. She stretched her arms and flexed her fingers. They could get so cramped. She rubbed the crick out of her neck. Smiling, she realized she wasn't as young as she used to be. Time was, she could sew all day. Well, before she had Henry, that is!

∽ Rail Fence Log Cabin ∽

Made by Karen Murphy, 74¼" x 89¾"; quilted by Ann Trotter

I find it hard to imagine the hours it took Abby to piece a quilt by hand when I can zip my fabric through a sewing machine. I'm grateful for the time my machine saves as I think of all the additional quilts I'm able to make. Quick to machine piece, the Rail Fence Log Cabin is a variation of a traditional Log Cabin block, created by moving the center hearth square to the very outside corner and building logs on only two sides. The result looks much like a Rail Fence quilt, but has blue squares zigzagging down the rows. If our Abby were alive today, she might recognize the fabrics in this quilt, because I used Civil War reproduction prints.

BLOCK NAME: Rail Fence Log Cabin
FINISHED BLOCK SIZE: 7¾" x 7¾"
SKILL LEVEL: Intermediate

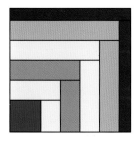

Materials

Yardages are based on 42"-wide fabric.
- 2¼ yards of brown floral for borders and binding
- 1¾ yards of cream print for blocks
- 1¾ yards of light brown print for blocks and middle border
- 1⅝ yards of red print for blocks and middle border
- 1⅜ yards of green print for blocks and middle border
- ⅞ yard of blue print for blocks and middle border
- 5⅞ yards of backing
- 80" x 100" piece of batting (queen)

Cutting

Fabric	First Cut	Second Cut
Cream	30 strips, 1¾" x 42"	From 4 of the strips, cut 63 rectangles, 1¾" x 2½". From 7 of the strips, cut 63 rectangles, 1¾" x 3¾". From 8 of the strips, cut 63 rectangles, 1¾" x 5". From 11 of the strips, cut 63 rectangles, 1¾" x 6¼".
Blue	4 strips, 2½" x 42"	Cut 63 squares, 2½" x 2½".
	7 strips, 2" x 42"	
Green	15 strips, 1¾" x 42"	From 7 of the strips, cut 63 rectangles, 1¾" x 3¾". From 8 of the strips, cut 63 rectangles, 1¾" x 5".
	7 strips, 2" x 42"	
Light brown	24 strips, 1¾" x 42"	From 11 of the strips, cut 63 rectangles, 1¾" x 6¼". From 13 of the strips, cut 63 rectangles, 1¾" x 7½".
	7 strips, 2" x 42"	
Red	29 strips, 1¼" x 42"	From 13 of the strips, cut 63 rectangles, 1¼" x 7½". From 16 of the strips, cut 63 rectangles, 1¼" x 8¼".
	7 strips, 2" x 42"	
Brown floral	16 strips, 3" x 42"	
	9 strips, 2½" x 42"	

Block Construction

Blocks are made using modified Log Cabin piecing. (See "Traditional Log Cabin Construction" on page 14.)

1. Sew each 1¾" x 2½" cream rectangle to one side of a 2½" blue square. Press toward the cream rectangles. Make 63 units.

Make 63.

2. Sew a 1¾" x 3¾" cream rectangle to each unit made in step 1 as shown. Press toward the newly added cream rectangles. Be careful to add the second log to the same side of each block so that all your blocks will look identical.

3. Continue sewing logs to just these two sides, following the order in the illustration. Press all seams toward the new logs. Make 63 blocks.

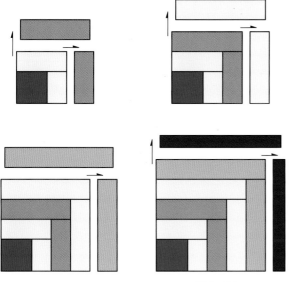

Make 63.

4. Square up the blocks to 8¼". (See "Squaring Up Blocks" on page 18.)

Quilt Assembly

1. Arrange seven blocks into a row as shown. Sew the blocks together. Repeat to make nine rows. Press all the seams in the same direction.

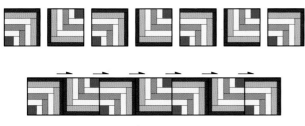

Make 9 rows.

2. Arrange the rows, rotating every other row 180° as shown. Sew the rows together. Press.

3. Sew 2" x 42" strips of red, green, blue, and brown together along the long edges. Press. Repeat to make seven strip sets.

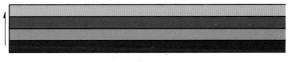

Make 7 strip sets.

4. From the strip sets, cut 54 segments, 5" wide.

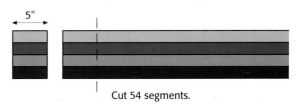

5"

Cut 54 segments.

5. Sew 12 units from step 4 together end to end to make the middle top border. Repeat to make the middle bottom border. Sew 15 units together to make a middle side border. Repeat to make a second middle side border. Press.

Top or bottom border.
Make 2.

Side border.
Make 2.

6. Sew the 3"-wide brown floral strips together end to end to make one long strip. From the strip, cut two lengths 64" for the inner top and bottom borders, two lengths 78" for the outer top and bottom borders, two lengths 79½" for the inner side borders, and two lengths 93½" for the outer side borders.

7. Sew together the strips from steps 5 and 6 to make the top, bottom, and side border units. (See "Mitered-Corner Borders" on page 22.) Press.

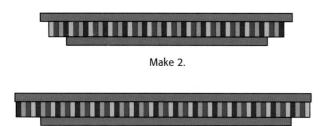

Make 2.

Make 2.

8. Working from the wrong side of the quilt, square up the corners with your ruler and rotary cutter. Make a mark ¼" from each corner.

9. Mark the center of each border unit and the center of each side of the quilt top. Pin the borders to the quilt top, matching the centers. Sew the borders to the quilt, stopping and backstitching at the ¼" mark on each corner. Be careful not to catch the border from another side in your seam.

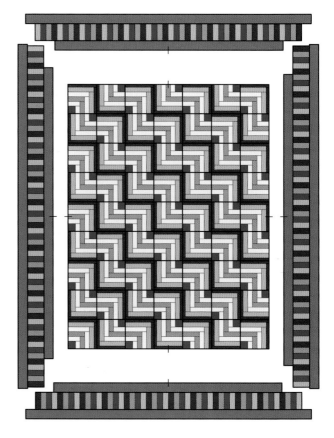

10. Miter the corners, being careful to cut and stitch accurately. Match the brown floral seams at the corners, but don't worry about matching the colors in the pieced bars of the middle border.

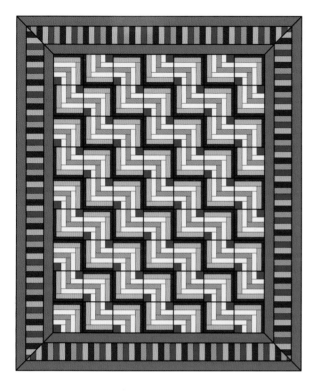

Finishing

1. Your quilt top is complete, and it's time to sandwich it with backing and batting. (Refer to "Layering" on page 24.) Quilt either by machine or by hand. The center of my quilt is machine quilted to echo the stipple design in the cream fabric. Tall loops are quilted in each bar of the middle border and a chain of flowers in each of the green borders. Trim excess batting and backing from the edges.

2. Piece the 2½"-wide brown floral strips end to end to make one long binding strip. Fold the strip in half lengthwise, wrong sides together, and press. Sew the raw edges of the binding to the front of your quilt. Fold the binding over to the back and hand stitch. (See "Binding" on page 24.)

Chapter 4

Abby sat at the table, wearing her woolen skirts. George was pacing the room back and forth till she thought she would scream. Every third pass, he'd stop and look out the window.

"It looks like snow, Abby, I think we should stay home." His forehead wrinkled with worry.

She wasn't about to be taken in by this. This was the third time she'd put on her woolens. "Just make a decision, dear. Stay or go."

He paused by the window again, squinting against the light. "Well, I do see some blue sky over there." He paused again. "All right, let's go!"

"Are you sure?" Abby grinned.

He turned to look at her. "What do you mean, am I . . . ?" his voice trailed off as he noted the playfulness in her eyes. "Been that bad, have I?"

"Yes, dear."

"Don't go giving me the 'yes dear' treatment!" They both laughed as they left the cabin—Abby with her sewing basket, her dish of venison stew, and some stones warmed in the stove for their feet, and George with a bundle of quilts and elk robes for them to wrap up in.

The weather for the trip to town turned lovely. The blue sky George had seen from a distance eventually chased the clouds away. He dropped Abby at the church and went on to the general store for their winter supplies.

Abby climbed the church steps, lugging her basket and eager to participate. She entered the building, quickly closing the door to keep out the cold air. Ladies were sitting around the quilt frame, taking their small stitches, laughing and visiting. She recognized some of them from the cabin raising.

"Hello!" Abby smiled. She set her dish of stew on the table with the other dishes.

"Abby, hello! I'm glad you made it." Mary got up, giving her a small hug. "Come and sit by me."

The chatter flowed seamlessly as Abby got out her needle and thimble. Someone passed her the thread, and she entered into the quilting.

Mary leaned over and whispered, "Do you know who that is? In the brown dress?"

Abby shook her head slightly.

"Mrs. Lewis. I hear your son is courting Rebecca. That true?"

Abby nodded her head this time, and eyed Mrs. Lewis.

"Well, I just hope he knows what he's getting into." Mary leaned back into her chair. Abby looked at her, a question in her eyes. Mary only nodded every so slightly as if to say, "Just watch her."

Abby kept her eyes on the quilt in front of her and her ears open, but it was hard to

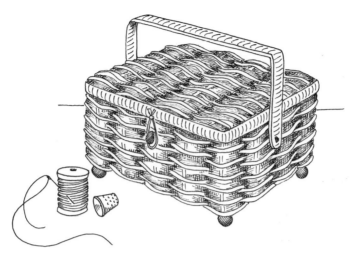

hear. Mrs. Lewis sat across the quilt from her and snatches of conversation floated around, obscuring any words Mrs. Lewis might be saying.

"My little Grace is walking now," a proud voice said.

"I heard that Susanna James went out walking with Jeremiah Taylor on Saturday. Did you know that? I wonder if her mother knows?"

"My recipe for sour cream cake has just disappeared! And right after Anna left on Thursday. I don't mean to imply . . . " the voice was drowned out by another.

"Of all the nerve! If he thinks he's good enough for my daughter . . . "

Abby glanced up without moving her head. Yes, that was Mrs. Lewis. Her heart sank as she realized the woman was speaking of Henry. Good enough!

"We've told him she is not interested in him and not to come again. But every night he comes. She's speaking to him only to be polite, you know." Mrs. Lewis paused to take a breath and, straightening up, stretched her cramped muscles. As she sat up, she

noticed Abby across the quilt. Abby looked up and they locked eyes. Just as quickly Mrs. Lewis looked away, but she never spoke of Henry again.

So, that's the way the wind blows, is it? My son isn't good enough for that hoyden of a daughter of hers? Abby's thoughts raced and she carefully concealed the anger in her face. She looked over at Mary, and Mary gave her a look that said, "See?" Some of the joy of the day was gone. Lunch passed and Abby didn't know what she ate.

"Come on Abby, forget it. That woman doesn't have a kind word to say about anyone," Mary said.

"It just makes me so mad! And it's not exactly like her daughter is a prize either, you know." Abby gave a hard sigh.

"Don't make me sorry I pointed her out to you," Mary threatened, smiling. "This is the first quilting bee you've been to, and the last one before winter. Enjoy it!"

"Mary, I'm sorry. You are so right. I won't let her ruin my day," Abby agreed with her friend.

Cornerstone

Made and quilted by Karen Murphy, 37" x 44¾"

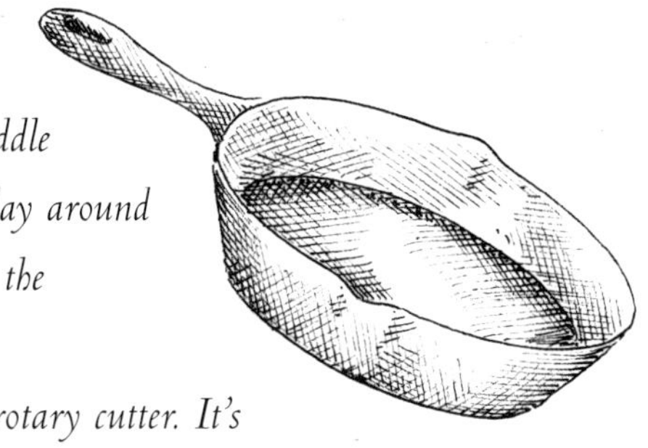

J ust as Abby heard fractured bits of conversation around the quilt frame, this quilt is built from "fractured" Log Cabin blocks. I put the "center" of the block in the middle of one side and visually cut the block in half. Arrange your blocks like my sample or play around with them and make your own design. You will find many new patterns depending on the number and placement of your colors, and how you position your blocks.

There are no templates for this quilt; all the angles are cut using your ruler and rotary cutter. It's quick and easy! But this quilt does have one important rule you need to follow: All the strips must be right side up when you cut the angle on the ends. *If they are not right side up, the angle will slant the wrong direction.*

BLOCK NAME: Fractured Log Cabin
FINISHED BLOCK SIZE: 7¾" x 7¾"
SKILL LEVEL: Intermediate

Materials

Yardages are based on 42"-wide fabric.

- ⋄ 1⅛ yards of blue floral for blocks, border, and binding
- ⋄ ⅝ yard of red floral for blocks and border
- ⋄ ⅝ yard of dark blue tone-on-tone for blocks
- ⋄ ⅜ yard of gold tone-on-tone for blocks
- ⋄ ⅜ yard of green floral for blocks
- ⋄ ⅜ yard of dark purple tone-on-tone for blocks
- ⋄ ¼ yard of light green tone-on-tone for blocks
- ⋄ ¼ yard of light purple tone-on-tone for blocks
- ⋄ 1⅝ yards of backing
- ⋄ 42" x 50" piece of batting (crib)

Cutting

Fabric	First Cut	Second Cut
Blue floral	7 strips, 1⅞" x 42"	From 3 of the strips, cut 20 rectangles, 1⅞" x 5⅛".
		From 3½ of the strips, cut 20 rectangles, 1⅞" x 6⅜".
	5 strips, 2" x 42"	
	5 strips, 2½" x 42"	
Dark blue	8 strips, 1⅞" x 42"	From 4 of the strips, cut 20 rectangles, 1⅞" x 6½".
		From 4 of the strips, cut 20 rectangles, 1⅞ x 7¾".
Green floral	4 strips, 1⅞" x 42"	Cut 20 rectangles, 1⅞" x 6½".
Light green	3 strips, 1⅞" x 42"	Cut 20 rectangles, 1⅞" x 5⅛".
Red floral	5 strips, 1⅞" x 42"	Cut 20 rectangles, 1⅞" x 9½".
	4 strips, 1½" x 42"	
Dark purple	4 strips, 1⅞" x 42"	Cut 20 rectangles, 1⅞" x 6¾".
Gold	5 squares, 5¼" x 5¼"	Cut each square twice diagonally to make 20 triangles. ⊠
	10 squares, 2⅞" x 2⅞"	Cut each square once diagonally to make 20 triangles. ◺
Light purple	10 squares, 2⅞" x 2⅞"	Cut each square once diagonally to make 20 triangles. ◺

Block Construction

Blocks are made using modified Log Cabin piecing. (See "Traditional Log Cabin Construction" on page 14.)

1. Stack four or five of the 1⅞" x 5⅛" blue floral rectangles on top of each other on your cutting mat. Be certain the right sides are all facing up and the edges match.

2. Place your ruler on top of the fabric stack, angling the top of the ruler to the right so the 45° line on the ruler aligns with the top of the fabric and the edge of the ruler touches the upper-right corner of the rectangle. Cut along the edge of the ruler. Discard the trimmed triangles. Repeat with the remaining 1⅞" x 5⅛" blue floral rectangles. You can cut four to eight pieces at a time.

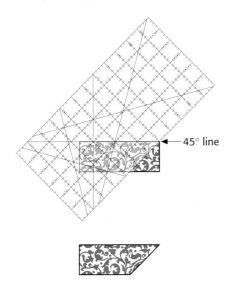

3. Trim the 7¾"-long dark blue, the 6½"-long green floral, and the 5⅛"-long light green rectangles in the same manner.

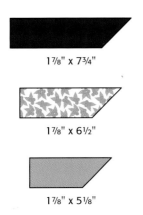

1⅞" x 7¾"

1⅞" x 6½"

1⅞" x 5⅛"

4. Stack four or five 1⅞" x 6⅜" blue floral rectangles with the right sides facing up and edges matching. Place your ruler on top of the fabric stack, angling the ruler to the left so the 45° line on the ruler aligns with the bottom of the fabric and the edge of the ruler touches the lower-right corner of the rectangle. Cut along the edge of the ruler. Discard the trimmed triangles. This will trim the rectangles with an angle slanting in the opposite direction from those cut in step 2. Repeat with the remaining 1⅞" x 6⅜" blue floral rectangles and the dark blue 6½"-long rectangles.

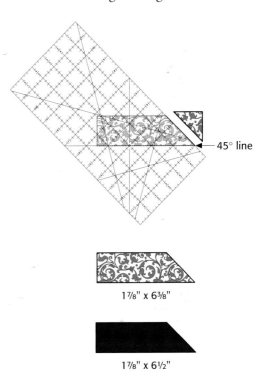

1⅞" x 6⅜"

1⅞" x 6½"

5. Trim the red floral rectangles and the dark purple rectangles on both ends—one end in one direction and the other end in the opposite direction. Be very careful that you trim the angles in the correct directions.

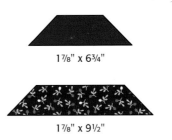

1⅞" x 6¾"

1⅞" x 9½"

6. Arrange one of each size and color of the trimmed pieces along with a gold 5¼" triangle, a gold 2⅞" triangle, and a light purple 2⅞" triangle into a block as shown.

7. With right sides together and the 90° corners matching, sew the 1⅞" x 5⅛" blue floral piece to the gold 5¼" triangle. Be careful to sew it to the side indicated in the art below. Press toward the blue floral.

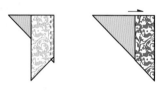

☙

The pieces all have at least one bias edge, which will easily stretch out of shape if handled too vigorously. It is especially important to press gently with an up-and-down motion instead of sliding the iron sideways across the fabric. Handle the edges as little as possible.

☙

8. With right sides together and the 90° corners matching, sew the 1⅞" x 6⅜" blue floral piece to the left side of the triangle unit as shown. Press toward the blue floral.

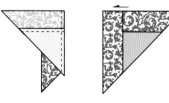

9. Repeating the technique described in steps 7 and 8, sew the dark blue pieces to the unit from step 8 as shown. Press toward the dark blue.

10. Sew the green floral piece, the light green piece, and the light purple triangle to one side of the unit from step 9 as shown. Press away from the dark blue. If the ends of your strips are a little ragged, trim them even with the long dark blue edges.

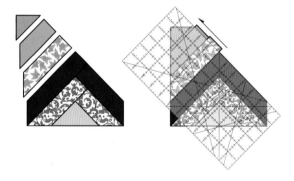

11. Sew the red floral piece, the dark purple piece, and the remaining gold triangle to the unit. Press away from the center of the block. Repeat steps 6–11 to make 20 blocks.

Make 20.

12. Square the blocks to 8¼". (See "Squaring Up Blocks" on page 18.)

Quilt Assembly

1. Arrange the blocks into five rows of four blocks each. You may follow the diagram below and rotate the blocks the same way I did or experiment with rotating them in different directions. The look of your quilt will change dramatically depending on how you orient the blocks.

2. Sew the blocks into rows. Press in the opposite direction from row to row. Sew the rows together. Press.

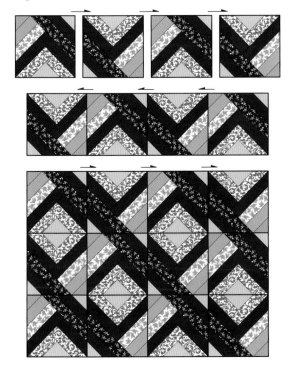

3. Measure the center of the quilt from top to bottom to determine the side border measurements. Cut two borders from the 1½" x 42" red floral strips to this measurement and sew them to the left and right sides of the quilt top. (See "Butted-Corner Borders" on page 21.) Press toward the borders.

4. Measure the center of the quilt from left to right to determine the top and bottom border measurements. Cut two borders from the 1½" x 42" red floral strips to this measurement and sew them to the top and bottom of the quilt top. Press toward the borders.

5. Repeat steps 3 and 4 to make outer borders from the 2" x 42" blue floral strips. Depending on the usable width of your fabric, you may need to piece strips end to end to yield enough length for the side borders. Press toward the blue borders.

Finishing

1. Your quilt top is complete, and it's time to sandwich it with backing and batting. (Refer to "Layering" on page 24.) Quilt either by machine or by hand. I quilted my quilt by machine, using in-the-ditch stitching for all the strips and a loopy design in the borders. Trim excess batting and backing from the edges.

2. Piece the 2½"-wide blue floral strips end to end to make one long binding strip. Fold the strip in half lengthwise, wrong sides together, and press. Sew the raw edges of the binding to the front of your quilt. Fold the binding over to the back and hand stitch. (See "Binding" on page 24.)

Chapter 5

Abby spread the red-and-white gingham over the tabletop, remembering the disagreement. George thought the purchase of fabric was a complete waste of money. Why cover the windows out here in the middle of the woods? Didn't Abby ask for windows so the cabin wouldn't be so dark? She smiled as the fabric smoothed under her fingers. The windows were measured, and she cut the appropriate pieces. George didn't understand her need for beauty in their home. The quilts he understood—they kept everyone warm. But curtains? When Abby wanted to buy fabric for curtains during their last trip to town, he had simply shaken his head and headed for the wagon to wait for her. After he left the store, she ordered enough gingham to make a tablecloth as well. And there would be scraps left for her Log Cabin quilt, which was turning out even better than expected.

In the wagon on the way home, Abby slipped her arm through his. "George, I know you don't understand about the curtains, but things like that are important to a woman." She laid her head on his shoulder.

"Nope, I don't understand. Seems like a perfect waste of hard-earned money to me. I thought you'd want the light in the room. Whadya want the windows for anyway?" He kept his eyes on the team.

"I love the windows for the light they let in. I want the curtains to make the room look cozy. Remember, we had curtains in Boston?"

"Well, yeah we did, but we had neighbors, too. Here, we don't have neighbors for miles."

"Curtains are for more than privacy. You'll see." She smiled up at him. He shook his head but gave her a slight grin from the side of his mouth.

Abby smiled at the remembrance and gathered her pieces of gingham, folded them and placed them in her sewing basket, and headed outside to the porch with the basket. She sat in her rocker hemming the edges of the fabric. It was a beautiful day, one of the few warm days left before winter chilled the air. The sun shone through the pines. Small dust motes floated lazily down the sunbeams. Warm pine sap scented the air and birds sang cheerfully from their branches.

Soon the snows would fall. In the back of her mind Abby knew there was still much to do to prepare for winter, but she pushed the thought away and determined to enjoy her afternoon of sewing.

That evening, her curtains hung at the windows. The tablecloth, although unhemmed, covered the smooth wood of their table. Abby placed the newly cleaned and polished oil lamp in the center of the table. The smell of baked beans and cornbread filled the cabin. The coffee bubbled on the back of the stove. She couldn't keep the

smile from her face. Abby eagerly waited for the reaction and understanding of her husband. Their cabin was warm and inviting, exactly the way she had envisioned it.

Abby heard George and their sons coming in from the barn for the evening meal. She heard bits of conversation relating to the butchering they'd done with their neighbor, who wouldn't be invited back next year because he didn't pull his weight, and the probability of getting a new iron cauldron. They stomped the dirt from their boots on the front porch and entered the cabin, still talking of butchering.

Abby served baked beans and large chunks of hot cornbread dripping with butter onto each plate. Her smile was bright, and she kissed George's cheek as he reached for his coffee. They sat down together. After George said the blessing, the three men dug into their food as if they hadn't eaten for days. George loved his grown sons, listening

intently to their thoughts and suggestions about developing the land. The talk flowed, laughter roared at jokes told, and a general contentment shone from each man's eyes. Yet, still not a word about the curtains.

Abby's smile dimmed.

"You know, those were the best baked beans you've ever made. Thanks." George reached over and touched her hand.

"Ma, got any more of those beans? They just taste extra good tonight, like Pa said. Whadya put in em?" Henry asked, grinning.

"They're the same beans I make all the time, but thank you."

It was then she realized that it wasn't the baked beans that were better—it was the atmosphere created by the new curtains and tablecloth. Abby's smile returned. As she cleared dishes from the table, George caught her eye and winked, continuing the butchering conversation as if nothing had happened.

Fancy Cabin

Made and quilted by Cathy Dahl, 41" x 49"

Glass windows were considered a luxury on the frontier, and the addition of curtains and a tablecloth "fancied up" Abby's home considerably. Like Abby's home, a Log Cabin block can be "fancied up" by adding more pieces of fabric! For this design, I set the log-cabin unit on point in the center of the block, and added triangles to the corners to create a secondary design when the blocks are set together. Many other designs will also work well in the corner areas.

BLOCK NAME: Fancy Cabin
FINISHED BLOCK SIZE: 8" x 8"
SKILL LEVEL: Intermediate

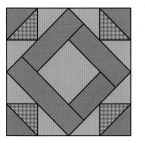

Materials

Yardages are based on 42"-wide fabric.
- 1¼ yards of tan print for blocks and middle border
- 1¼ yards of pink print for blocks, inner and outer borders, and binding
- ¾ yard of green print for blocks
- ½ yard of pink plaid for blocks
- 3 yards of backing
- 46" x 54" piece of batting (crib)

Cutting

Fabric	First Cut	Second Cut
Tan	2 strips, 3⅜" x 42"	20 squares, 3⅜" x 3⅜"
	6 to 7* strips, 2⅞" x 42"	80 squares, 2⅞" x 2⅞". Cut each square once diagonally to make 160 triangles. △
	4 to 5* strips, 2½" x 42"	
Green	5 strips, 1⅞" x 42"	From 2 of the strips, cut 20 rectangles, 1⅞" x 3⅜". From 2½ of the strips, cut 20 rectangles, 1⅞" x 4¾".
	3 to 4* strips, 2⅞" x 42"	40 squares, 2⅞" x 2⅞". Cut each square once diagonally to make 80 triangles. △
Pink print	6 strips, 1⅞" x 42"	From 2½ of the strips, cut 20 rectangles, 1⅞" x 4¾". From 3½ of the strips, cut 20 rectangles, 1⅞" x 6⅛".
	9 strips, 1½" x 42"	
	5 strips, 2½" x 42"	
Pink plaid	3 to 4* strips, 2⅞" x 42"	40 squares, 2⅞" x 2⅞". Cut each square once diagonally to make 80 triangles. △

*The number of strips you need to cut will depend on the usable width of your fabric. By the time you cut off the selvages, many fabrics are closer to 40" wide than 42" wide, and that can make quite a difference! Start by cutting the smaller number of strips. If you can't cut enough pieces from those strips, you will need to cut the larger number of strips.

Block Construction

1. Arrange a 3⅜" tan square, one green rectangle of each size, and one pink rectangle of each size as shown.

2. Sew according to the traditional Log Cabin method. (See "Traditional Log Cabin Construction" on page 14.) Press away from the tan square. Square up the unit to 6⅛". (See "Squaring Up Blocks" on page 18.) Repeat to make 20 center units.

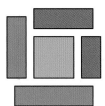

6⅛"

Center unit.
Make 20.

3. Sew a green triangle and a plaid triangle together as shown to make a triangle square. (Be careful not to stretch the triangles when you sew this seam. The bias edges make the triangles very stretchy.) Press toward the green triangle. Repeat to make 80 triangle squares.

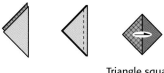

Triangle square.
Make 80.

4. Sew tan triangles to the two plaid sides of a triangle square as shown. Press seams toward the tan fabric. Make 80 corner units.

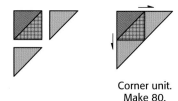

Corner unit.
Make 80.

5. Sew the corner units to Log Cabin center units to make 20 Fancy Cabin blocks. Press.

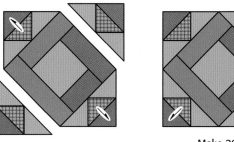

Make 20.

6. Square up your blocks so they measure 8½".

Quilt Assembly

1. Arrange the blocks into five rows of four blocks each. I chose a layout with the pink logs on the left side of each block, but you can experiment with different placements. Sew the blocks into rows. Press in the

opposite direction from row to row. Sew the rows together. Press.

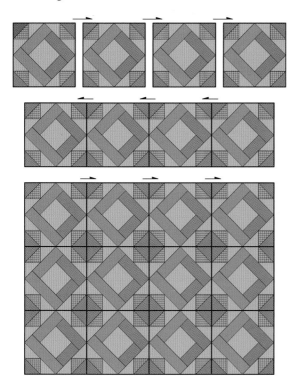

2. Measure the center of the quilt from top to bottom to determine the side border measurements. Cut two borders from the 1½" x 42" pink strips to this measurement and sew them to the left and right sides of the quilt top. (See "Butted-Corner Borders" on page 21.) Press toward the borders.

3. Measure the center of the quilt from left to right to determine the top and bottom border measurements. Cut two borders from the 1½" x 42" pink strips to this measurement and sew them to the top and bottom of the quilt top. Press toward the borders.

4. Repeat steps 2 and 3 to make middle borders from the 2½" x 42" tan strips. Press toward the tan borders.

5. Repeat steps 2 and 3 to make outer borders from the remaining 1½" x 42" pink strips. Press toward the outer pink borders.

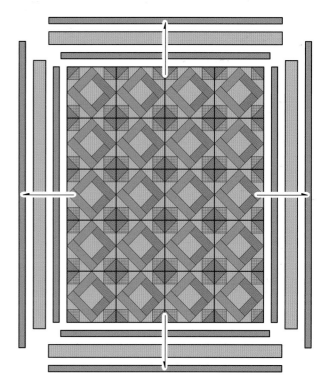

Finishing

1. Your quilt top is complete, and it's time to sandwich it with backing and batting. (Refer to "Layering" on page 24.) Quilt either by machine or by hand. My quilt was quilted by machine with flower motifs in the center of each Log Cabin and a square-in-a-square secondary pattern. The tan border features a continuous-line flower-and-leaf design, while continuous-line leaves grace the pink borders. Trim excess batting and backing from the edges.

2. Piece the 2½"-wide pink strips end to end to make one long binding strip. Fold the strip in half lengthwise, wrong sides together, and press. Sew the raw edges of the binding to the front of your quilt. Fold the binding over to the back and hand stitch. (See "Binding" on page 24.)

Chapter 6

ABBY SAT next to George in the small church pew. Henry and Rebecca stood in front of the preacher, their backs to the congregation. The preacher was particularly long-winded today, and Abby felt like she'd been sitting for hours. She'd seen George glance out the window several times, checking for snow. It was late in the year, and bitterly cold. Today the clouds were hanging low and full, and you could smell snow coming. The preacher seemed oblivious to the fact that most of these people had quite a ride home today. Getting caught in the snow was dangerous and deadly.

She breathed a sigh of relief as the preacher put his final blessing on the couple, and Henry and Rebecca turned and walked down the aisle as husband and wife. Henry was red-faced and stiff as a board. Rebecca was smiling ear to ear and glowing with young beauty. Tears threatened to fill Abby's eyes as she realized, again, that her son belonged to another woman. Would she ever get used to this?

Mr. and Mrs. Lewis nodded stiffly to Abby and George as they met in the aisle. Curt greetings were exchanged and the parents of the bride moved on. As if they were nothing more than acquaintances!

"George! What is wrong with those people?" Abby whispered, at the same time smiling cordially to the others gathered around to offer congratulations to the parents.

George gave her a small eye roll, and shrugged his shoulders slightly as if to say, "Durned if I know!"

Mary came up to her with a hug. "Don't pay any attention to those two. They're like that with just about everybody. If she doesn't have something bad to say, she doesn't say anything at all."

They made their way through the crowd, everybody heading for their wagons. The ride loomed ahead and they were eager to get home before the snow flew. Wedding presents had been taken to the new cabin last week. The young couple was eager to be rid of the crowd and head to their own home for the first time. One by one, the wagons headed out in different directions, all trying to beat the storm.

George, Abby, and Samuel crowded together on the seat of the wagon. It was easier to keep warm this way. They wrapped themselves in elk robes and wool scarves and hats. Mittens of wool and leather protected their hands from the bitter wind. With no stove-warmed stones for this trip, they had to pay careful attention to their feet. Frostbite was a real concern. Every half hour or so, George reminded them all to stamp their feet to get the blood flowing again.

Soon, tiny flakes of snow began to appear. George groaned as he urged the

horses to a faster pace. They still had more than half the distance between them and home. The wind picked up a little and the wool scarves around their necks flapped in response, often hitting the person next to them in the face. The gusts began swirling around them, making little funnels with the snow. Abby huddled into her elk robe and pulled her wool scarf over her face entirely. She nodded at Samuel to do the same. George had his scarf pulled right up to his eyes.

Abby prayed they would reach home safely.

The flakes grew larger. The wind howled even louder. She was cold to the bone, despite all the wrappings. She began to shiver and knew that was a bad sign. She stomped her feet even before receiving a reminder from George. She unwrapped her arms, which were hugging her body for warmth, and clapped her hands together. The muffled sound could barely be heard.

Then, suddenly, the wind stopped. The snow ceased its swirling and dancing, and began to plummet steadily to the ground. Although grateful for the abatement of the wind, Abby knew this presented another danger. At the rate the snow was falling, it would soon be too deep for the horses to pull the wagon. The family might have to walk the rest of the way. George pulled the reins to stop the horses. Abby looked at him in surprise, pulling down her scarf. She'd expected him to urge them to go faster.

"Come on, get down. Samuel, unhook the harnesses. We're going to leave the wagon here and ride the horses home. Yes, just leave the bridle on. Hurry!" Quickly they unhooked the wagon and hopped up on the horses, riding them bareback. George helped Abby onto the back of his horse. Oh, the blessed warmth of the horse! Abby smiled as she laid her head on her husband's broad back. They would be home any time now.

Designing Your Own
∽ Secondary Pattern ∽

*A*bby and George had to find creative solutions to the problems they met on the frontier. Show some pioneering spirit of your own and create an entirely new block by tweaking a traditional Log Cabin design. Changing the color, size, and placement of the center square, or "hearth," can create many variations, while playing with the shape or placement of one or more of the "logs" offers even more options.

In "Fancy Cabin," shown on page 62, I made a "small" Log Cabin—that is, with only one set of logs around the center square. I placed the log-cabin unit on point in the middle of the block and, instead of using one large triangle in each corner, I pieced a corner unit out of four smaller triangles. This time, let's choose a different approach for the corner units. Now it's your turn to play with fabric and come up with your own block design.

Materials

- Several sharpened pencils
- Good eraser
- Tablet of graph paper, 4 squares to the inch
- Ruler
- Colored pencils
- Adhesive tape
- Scissors
- Freezer paper

Designing a Straight-Set Block

1. Draw an 8" square on a sheet of graph paper. Divide the square in half horizontally and vertically with two dashed lines. These lines indicate the midpoint of each side.

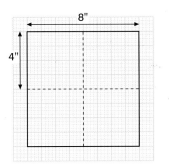

2. Using the dashed lines for reference, draw a 2" square in the center of the 8" square. This represents the center of your Log Cabin block. The square will extend 1" above and below the horizontal dashed line and 1" on either side of the vertical dashed line.

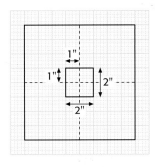

3. Draw 1½"-wide rectangular "logs" on all four sides of the center square.

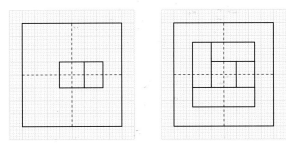

4. The center of the block is now filled in, but we still have 1½" on every side to play with. Draw a square in each corner. This creates a design with a four-patch secondary pattern that will appear when four blocks are set together. You can now make duplicates of your square and use colored pencils (or different shadings with a regular pencil) to indicate where to place different fabrics. Use two different colors in the corners, to create four patches between the Log Cabins.

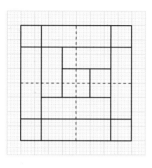

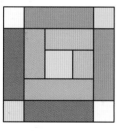

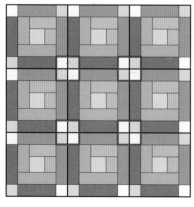

Four-patch secondary pattern

5. You can shade in several blocks, cut them out, and experiment. Try rotating the blocks in different directions, or ask yourself, how would your design look with sashing and cornerstones between the blocks? You don't have to commit your fabric—just draw it on graph paper!

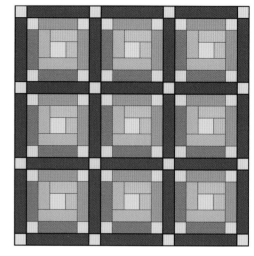

Blocks with sashing and cornerstones

6. Now try a few designs on your own. What if you changed the overall size to 12" and put Flying Geese blocks instead of sashing strips between the outer squares? Or, make the center square 4" and divide it into smaller designs. Once you start playing with paper and pencil, the ideas start coming faster than you can draw them! What if you moved your Log Cabin to one corner of the block? Wow! That leaves you a great area to play with—divide it up into a design that pleases you.

Designing a Block Set On Point

1. Draw a 10" square on a sheet of graph paper. (You may have to tape two pieces of paper together.) Divide the square as before with horizontal and vertical dashed lines through the center.

2. Connect the midpoints on each side to draw a square set on point in the middle of the 10" square. This will be the Log Cabin portion of your block.

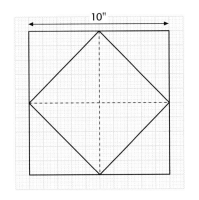

3. Add one round of logs inside the center square. The graph paper won't be much help measuring the width of the logs, so use a ruler to mark the width you want. This block will make a nice secondary pattern if you choose to make the corner triangles scrappy.

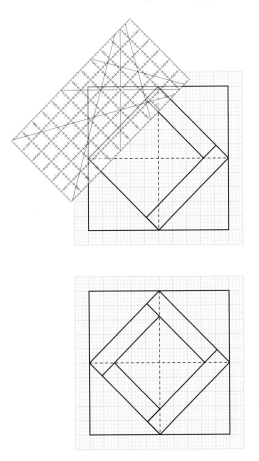

4. You could also make pinwheels by dividing the corner triangles in half.

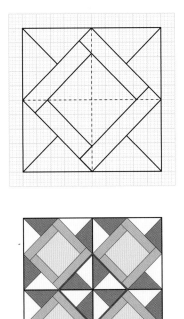

Pinwheel secondary pattern

5. Perhaps you'd like to try string piecing in the corners?

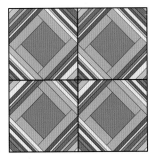

String-pieced corners

Block Construction

Once you find a design you like, it is time to make a test block to see how it will look in fabric. Your diagram represents the finished block, so each piece will need to have seam allowances added. Always calculate the size of the finished piece first; then add seam allowances. Most of the pieces in your block may be rotary cut; odd shapes may need templates.

Finished Diagonal Measurements

If you draw your block full-sized, you may find it easiest to simply use a ruler to measure the size of the finished pieces. Even so, there may be times when you need to calculate the diagonal length of a square. If the equation $a^2 + b^2 = c^2$ makes your eyes cross, have no fear. There is an easier way! Simply multiply the length of a side of the square by 1.414. For example, the diagonal length of a 3½" square would be 4.949". (3½" x 1.414 = 4.949") Since we are building quilts instead of bridges, round 4.949" to the nearest ⅛", or 5".

If you know the diagonal measurement and want to find what the side of a square measures, divide the diagonal measurement by 1.414. For example, a square set on point measures 8" from point to point. The side of the square would be (8" ÷ 1.414 = 5.66") about 5⅝".

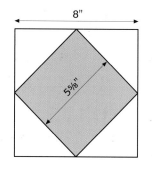

Calculating Cut Sizes

Square or rectangular pieces may be rotary cut. To figure rotary-cut sizes, measure the finished size of the piece and add ½" for the seam allowances (¼" on all four sides). For example: If the finished size is 1" square, cut 1½" x 1½". If the finished size is 1" x ¾", cut 1½" x 1¼".

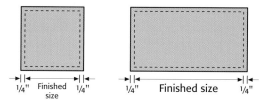

Triangles that have a 90° corner may be rotary cut from squares. There are two ways to cut this type of triangle. You can cut a square in half once on the diagonal (half-square triangle), or you may cut a larger square in quarters by making two diagonal cuts (quarter-square triangle). The triangles are the same shape, but they have different edges that are cut on the bias. How do you know which triangle to cut? Look at where it will be used in the block. It is usually best not to have the bias edge of a triangle on the outside edge of a block.

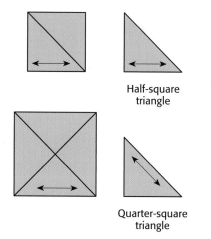

Half-square triangle

Quarter-square triangle

To calculate the size of the square needed to make half-square triangles, measure the length of one of the short sides of the triangle and add ⅞". To calculate the size of the square needed to make quarter-square triangles, measure the length of the long side of the triangle and add 1¼".

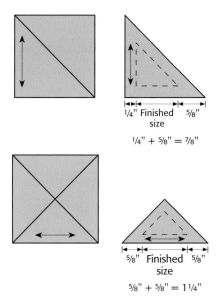

¼" Finished size 5/8"

¼" + 5/8" = 7/8"

5/8" Finished size 5/8"

5/8" + 5/8" = 1¼"

For odd shapes, or if you prefer to work with templates instead of rotary cutting, simply trace the piece onto freezer paper; then use a ruler to add a line ¼" outside all the edges. Cut out the shape on the outside line and use a low setting on your iron to lightly press the freezer-paper pattern to the right side of your fabric. Cut the shape from the fabric. Your freezer-paper pattern can be reused several times before it will no longer adhere to the fabric.

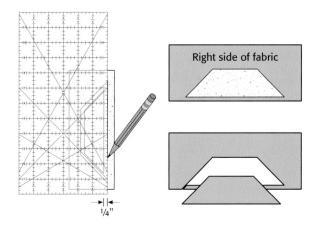

Right side of fabric

¼"

You may find it helpful to develop a good idea of what your quilt will look like before you start cutting fabric. If you have a design program on your computer, you can draw your block on the computer and ask for a quilt layout plan. You can also draw a quilt plan on your graph paper. For small quilts, use a scale of one square = 1". For larger quilts, use a scale of one square = 2" or 3".

Use your finished block size to decide whether to use two inches per square or three inches per square. If you're creating a 10" block, use two. Ten is divisible by two and you won't be as likely to have to deal with half squares on your graph paper. If the finished block is 9", use a scale of three inches to a square, since nine is divisible by three. You can use either scale for a 12" block.

Once you've selected and approved your design, go ahead and start cutting fabric! Sew and press your way to an original quilt. Here are some ideas to get you going:

- Vary the number of log rows to increase or decrease design room.
- What happens if your block is designed to be off-center?
- Try two different Log Cabin variations in one quilt, alternating the blocks.
- Try a two-color plan first, and then use the same block but lots of fabrics to make a quilt with a scrappy look. The two quilts will look entirely different!
- Make your logs skinny (under 1") or chunky (over 2"). Make some of your blocks over-sized (larger than 12").
- Experiment with different angles in your secondary design area. See how well they form a secondary pattern.
- Most importantly, have fun!

Chapter 7

WINTER HIT with a vengeance, demanding a steep price for every warm fall day. Every storm left deep drifts. George and Sam kept a path shoveled to the barn, and strung a rope from the front door to the barn door. Animals needed to be fed and watered even during blizzards when you couldn't see your hand in front of your face.

Winter was nearly as busy as summer. It was the time to make new tools, mend leather harnesses, build furniture. George and Sam spent much of their time in the barn, and Abby was left alone in the cabin. She cooked and cleaned the small living space, but it quickly became monotonous.

Planning to continue work on her new quilt, she gathered her pieces and sat in her rocking chair. Pine boughs sagged under the weight of heavy snow. Abby leaned her head against the back of her chair and closed her eyes, remembering.

Winters in Boston were just as snowy, but not nearly so lonely. Winter was a time for sleigh rides with friends, church socials, and quilting bees. She smiled as she remembered a church social three winters ago.

George had lashed bells to the horse's harness, and as they made their way through the snowy streets, jingling music announced their presence. Henry and Sam had gone ahead to meet the other young people, and Abby was alone with her husband. She tucked her hand in his warm pocket, preferring it to her fur muff. The streetlamps glowed warmly through the snowfall.

Inside the church, firelight glanced off the walls. Large tables were lined against one wall and covered with food of all kinds. The ladies of the church made gallons of coffee and filled earthenware crocks with the steaming brew. Other crocks contained hot apple cider. The scent of coffee and cinnamon wafted through the room. Laughter and voices filled every corner as friends greeted each other.

"May I have your attention please?" Reverend Goodwin's voice rose above the clamor. "Welcome!" His smile was infectious. "Welcome! It's so good to see all of you. I hope you have a chance to indulge yourself in all this delicious food." He swept his arm toward the tables. "After you've eaten your fill, we're going to help you run it off!" He laughed as people glanced at each other, puzzled. "Go on. Eat!" He shooed them away, grinning.

Abby and George filled their plates and spent the next 30 minutes or so eating and visiting with friends. Abby wore her new red wool dress trimmed with claret silk piping and cream lace. She knew it looked becoming on her, and she also knew that George was watching her.

"Folks, let's get those plates put away and come on over," Reverend Goodwin's voice boomed all too soon. He held out his arms to

beckon the crowd. "Ladies form a line on the right side of the room and gentlemen on the left side. Now, all of you line up against the sides. Yes, that's right." He guided and prodded them into position. "Lydia," he said, speaking to his wife, "You can come out now."

Lydia appeared, enjoying the suspense and the joke she shared with her husband. She carried a spoon and an egg.

"Here are the rules. Ladies, we'll start with you," the clergyman bowed in their direction, "Miss Holly, since you're first in line, take the spoon in your hand. Place the egg upon it and hand it off to the first gentleman in line. Oh, I forgot to mention! You have to walk backwards!" Groans were heard. "Then the gentleman will do the same, taking the egg back to the next lady in line. Once you've had your turn, you can cheer the others onward! Your teammates can help direct you, but you cannot turn around to look where you're going.

You must stop directly in front of the person at the head of the line. All right! Go!"

Oh, the laughing and shouting! The men made fun of Miss Holly's awkward attempt to deliver the egg to the first gentleman. After she finally handed off the fragile cargo to him, he took three steps, stumbled, fell down, and dropped the egg. They all gasped as the egg hit the floor, then laughed when they realized it was boiled. Lydia produced another egg and the race was on again.

Tears spilled down Abby's cheeks. How lonely she was for her friends, her family. She tried to prolong the memory but finally had to open her eyes. The snow continued to fall, but failed to provide the cheer it had in Boston. Abby got up to add another log to the fire. Back in her rocker, she picked up her quilt pieces but, for once, the rhythmic work of the needle failed to raise her spirits.

ᐁ Three Furrows ᐊ

Made by Karen Murphy, 45" x 57"; quilted by Mary Decker

Today, accustomed as we are to cell phones, email, freeways, and transcontinental flights, it is difficult to imagine the months of isolation settlers endured. In the dark of winter with the land buried under snow, Abby would have dreamed of spring and the sight of George plowing the first furrows in the field. She may have imagined how the deep brown soil would smell moist and rich, and would soon be tinged with a soft green haze. "Three Furrows" echoes this anticipation of spring with both color and design.

I started with a classic Log Cabin arrangement called "Straight Furrows." By using a third color on the last two logs in each block, I created a third furrow, adding a new twist to the traditional design.

Block name: Three Furrows
Finished block size: 11½" x 11½"
Skill level: Intermediate

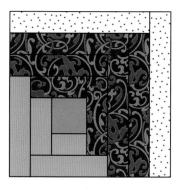

Materials

Yardages are based on 42"-wide fabric.

- ✧ 1½ yards of red paisley for blocks
- ✧ 1 yard of green tone-on-tone for blocks, border, and binding
- ✧ ¾ yard of red dot for blocks
- ✧ ¾ yard of light brown tone-on-tone for blocks
- ✧ 4 yards of backing
- ✧ 55" x 67" batting (twin)

Cutting

Fabric	First Cut	Second Cut
Green	2 strips, 3" x 42"	20 squares, 3" x 3"
	6 strips, 1½" x 42"	
	6 strips, 2½" x 42"	
Light brown	1 strip, 3" x 42"	20 rectangles, 2" x 3"
	1 strip, 4½" x 42"	20 rectangles, 2" x 4½"
	1 strip, 6" x 42"	20 rectangles, 2" x 6"
	1 strip, 7½" x 42"	20 rectangles, 2" x 7½"
Red paisley	1 strip, 4½" x 42"	20 rectangles, 2" x 4½"
	1 strip, 6" x 42"	20 rectangles, 2" x 6"
	1 strip, 7½" x 42"	20 rectangles, 2" x 7½"
	2 strips, 9" x 42"	40 rectangles, 2" x 9"
	1 strip, 10½" x 42"	20 rectangles, 2" x 10½"
Red dot	1 strip, 10½" x 42"	20 rectangles, 2" x 10½"
	1 strip, 12" x 42"	20 rectangles, 2" x 12"

Block Construction

Blocks are made using modified Log Cabin piecing. (See "Traditional Log Cabin Construction" on page 14.)

1. Arrange the pieces for one block as shown.

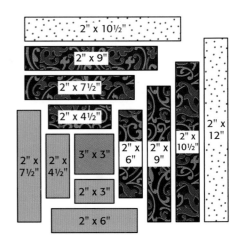

2. Start by sewing the 2" x 3" light brown rectangle to the green square. Press. Sew, in this order, the 2" x 4½" light brown rectangle, the 2" x 4½" red paisley rectangle, and the 2" x 6" red paisley rectangle to the green square. Press away from the square. The first round of logs is now complete.

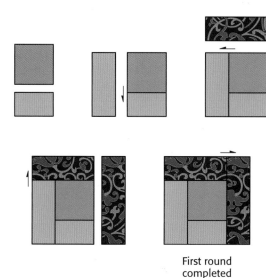

First round completed

3. Sew the second round of logs to the center unit as shown. Press away from the center.

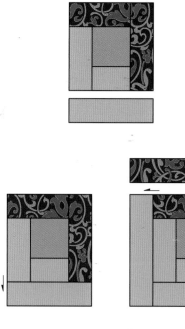

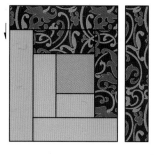

Second round completed

4. Sew a 2" x 9" red paisley rectangle to the unit. Be careful to add it to the correct side as illustrated below. Press away from the center of the block. Sew a 2" x 10½" red paisley rectangle to the unit, adding it to the correct side as illustrated. Press away from the center of the block.

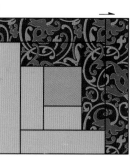

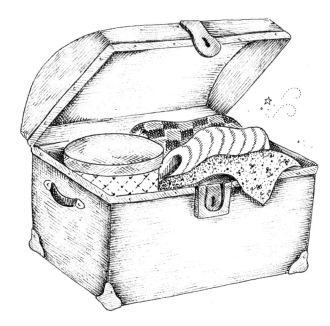

5. Sew the 2" x 10½" red dot rectangle to the shorter red paisley piece on the unit. Press toward the red dot. Sew the 2" x 12" red dot rectangle to the longer red paisley piece on the unit. Press toward the red dot. Repeat steps 1–5 to make 20 blocks.

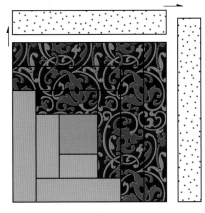

Make 20.

6. Square the blocks to 12". (See "Squaring Up Blocks" on page 18.)

Quilt Assembly

1. Arrange the blocks into five rows of four blocks each. Position the blocks the way I have or experiment with rotating the blocks in different directions.

2. Sew the blocks into rows. Press in the opposite direction from row to row. Sew the rows together. Press.

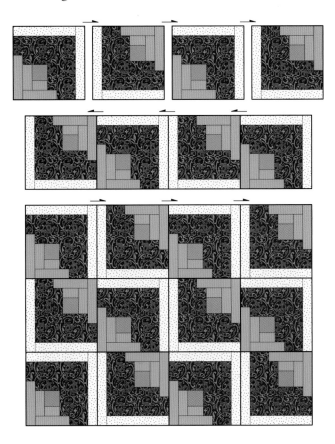

3. Measure the center of the quilt from top to bottom to determine the side border measurements. Cut two borders from the 1½" x 42" green strips to this measurement and sew them to the left and right sides of the quilt top. (See "Butted-Corner Borders" on page 21.) Press toward the borders.

4. Measure the center of the quilt from left to right to determine the top and bottom border measurements. Cut two borders from the 1½" x 42" green strips to this measurement and sew them to the top and bottom of the quilt top. Press toward the borders.

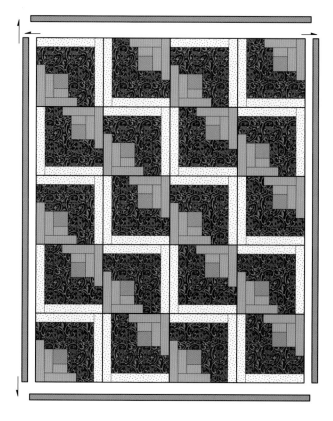

Finishing

1. Your quilt top is complete, and it's time to sandwich it with backing and batting. (Refer to "Layering" on page 24.) Quilt either by machine or by hand. This quilt was machine quilted with natural-colored thread in an allover loopy pattern. Trim excess batting and backing from the edges.

2. Piece the 2½"-wide green strips end to end to make one long binding strip. Fold the strip in half lengthwise, wrong sides together, and press. Sew the raw edges of the binding to the front of your quilt. Fold the binding over to the back and hand stitch. (See "Binding" on page 24.)

Chapter 8

Abby stood at the foot of the bed, admiring the completed Log Cabin quilt. It was unlike any other design she'd ever seen. After the snow melted, she'd take the quilt to the next bee.

The winter days had been long and dark. George and Samuel had taken a few hunting trips when the walls of the barn had closed in on them. But Abby was left to the cabin. Because she couldn't go anywhere, the Log Cabin quilt had grown larger every day.

Today the sun shone brightly, and icicles dripped from the eaves of the cabin. The breeze was warm, and the smell of spring was in the air.

"Abby!" George hollered from the barn.

Quickly she ran to the barn.

"A new calf!" George was grinning from ear to ear. "A little heifer too. Another milk cow is good news!"

"George, she's beautiful!" The calf nudged her nose between the slats of the stall in curiosity.

"Come on, we should leave them alone." George led Abby away, his arm around her shoulders.

"Let's stand out here in the sun for a minute. Doesn't it feel good?" Abby lifted her face to the sun and closed her eyes. "I'm so tired of being in the cabin, I could scream."

"Go get your coat. Let's go over to Henry's. I'm sure Rebecca is ready for a visit too."

Abby leaned over and kissed his cheek before fetching her coat.

The ride was lovely. The horses' hooves crunching through snow, combined with birdsong and the drip, drip of snow melting from trees created a symphony of spring. Though snow still covered the ground, the long winter days seemed to melt away in the presence of this beautiful preview of spring. Abby wanted to laugh, jump up and down, run and twirl, and throw her arms in the air in celebration. But the joy stayed inside, and she behaved like a proper lady.

George pulled up next to Henry's barn.

"Hello!" He called in a loud voice to announce their arrival.

Rebecca appeared at the front door. Her face was pale, her apron dirty. Brown hair hung lifeless from a bun on top of her head. The sparkle in her eyes was gone.

"Rebecca, dear! How are you?" Abby phrased her question diplomatically.

"Oh, fine." Unconsciously she smoothed her hair but didn't look Abby in the eyes. Abby and George exchanged a look of concern.

"Is Henry home?"

"He's been out huntin' since yesterday mornin'. Coffee?" Rebecca asked.

Carefully, Abby looked around the small room, not wanting Rebecca to notice and feel judged. Dishes had not been washed, nor clothes. The bed linens were rumpled

and strewn about, and the floor was gritty with dirt.

George excused himself to the barn, saying he'd check on the cow for Rebecca. After exchanging another look with Abby, he left the room.

Abby reached for Rebecca's hand. It was trembling. "Rebecca? Are you all right?" she spoke gently.

Tears puddled in Rebecca's eyes, and she covered her face with her hands. "It's just been awful! I cry all the time; Henry runs to the barn. There's no one to talk to and . . ." The words were muffled through her hands, and the sobs became louder. Abby quietly got up and began to straighten the room, letting Rebecca have her cry. Lord knows she'd had many of the same feelings.

After a few minutes, Rebecca dried her tears on a corner of her apron and sniffed, "I'm sure you must be terrible disappointed in me."

"No, dear, I'm not. I was just thinking I've had days like this myself."

"You have?" Rebecca said, surprised.

"Oh yes, every woman does. When the weather is bad, like it was this year, it's impossible for us to get out and keep each other company. Women need the company of other women, you know." Abby filled the dishpan with hot water from the stove and shaved some soap into it.

"I didn't realize. I thought I was a failure . . . as a wife." Rebecca looked ashamed.

"Oh, I don't believe that for one minute." Abby began to hum as she worked. The atmosphere began to change from one charged with tension to one infused with warmth. "I'll just do up these dishes real quick, and why don't you change clothes, comb your hair, and wash your face. You'll feel like a new woman."

Rebecca nodded and stepped behind a curtain strung across a corner of the room. A few minutes later she emerged wearing a red calico dress. "This used to be my favorite dress! I don't know why I quit wearing it." There was a little lilt in her voice as she combed through her hair.

The dishes done, the floor swept, and the bed straightened, Abby handed Rebecca her coat. "Let's leave a note for Henry. You're coming home with us. We've both been alone for too long." Rebecca smiled a tearful smile and gave Abby a hug.

"Thank you," Rebecca whispered.

❧ Triangle Swirls ❧

Made by Karen Murphy, 43¼" x 57¼"; quilted by Mary Decker

*I*nstead of four walls, what if your Log Cabin block has only three? There are no rules to say that the middle of the Log Cabin block has to be square! I chose to combat the winter doldrums with the bright purples and greens of spring, but this pattern will look terrific in almost any color scheme.

BLOCK NAME: Triangle Log Cabin
FINISHED BLOCK SIZE: 7¼" each side
SKILL LEVEL: Experienced

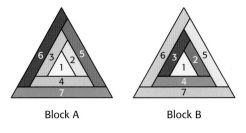

Block A   Block B

Materials

Yardages are based on 42"-wide fabric.

- 1⅜ yards of dark purple tone-on-tone for blocks, outer border, and binding
- 1⅛ yards of cream tone-on-tone for blocks and side and corner triangles
- 1 yard of dark green tone-on-tone for blocks and middle border
- ⅞ yard of dark blue tone-on-tone for blocks and inner border
- ¾ yard of light green tone-on-tone for blocks
- ⅝ yard of light purple tone-on-tone for blocks
- ⅝ yard of light blue tone-on-tone for blocks
- 3¼ yards of backing
- 54" x 68" piece of batting (twin)
- Freezer paper or template plastic

Cutting

Small and large triangle patterns are on pages 90–91.

Fabric	First Cut	Second Cut	Piece
Cream	5 strips, 3" x 42"	62 squares, 3" x 3"	Piece 1 (Blocks A, B)
	3 strips, 6⅞" x 42" (see cutting layout on page 86)	10 of large triangle template	Side triangle
		8 of small triangle template	Side triangle
		8 of small triangle template reversed	Side triangle
Light blue	10 strips, 1½" x 42"	31 rectangles, 1½" x 4"	Piece 2 (Block A)
		31 rectangles, 1½" x 6¾"	Piece 5 (Block B)
Light purple	11 strips, 1½" x 42"	31 rectangles, 1½" x 5"	Piece 3 (Block A)
		31 rectangles, 1½" x 7½"	Piece 6 (Block B)
Light green	13 strips, 1½" x 42"	31 rectangles, 1½" x 5¾"	Piece 4 (Block A)
		31 rectangles, 1½" x 8½"	Piece 7 (Block B)
Dark blue	10 strips, 1½" x 42"	31 rectangles, 1½" x 6¾"	Piece 5 (Block A)
		31 rectangles, 1½" x 4"	Piece 2 (Block B)
	6 strips, 1½" x 42"		Border
Dark purple	11 strips, 1½" x 42"	31 rectangles, 1½" x 7½"	Piece 6 (Block A)
		31 rectangles, 1½" x 5"	Piece 3 (Block B)
	6 strips, 1½" x 42"		Border
	6 strips, 2½" x 42"		Binding
Dark green	13 strips, 1½" x 42"	31 rectangles, 1½" x 8½"	Piece 7 (Block A)
		31 rectangles, 1½" x 5¾"	Piece 4 (Block B)
	6 strips 1½" x 42"		Border

Block Construction

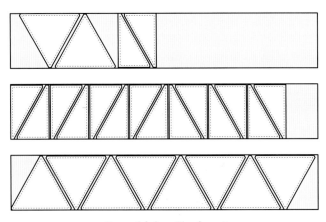
Cream fabric cutting layout

1. Make 62 copies of the foundation-piecing pattern on page 89.

2. Paper piece 31 of block A and 31 of block B, following the fabric placement in the cutting chart and referring to the illustrations on page 87. In block A, the first round of logs is light-colored and the second round of logs is dark-colored; in block B, the light and dark

values are reversed. (See "Paper Foundation Piecing" on page 16.)

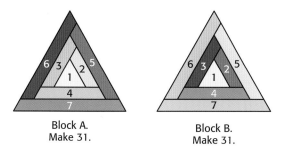

Block A.
Make 31.

Block B.
Make 31.

3. Trim the excess fabric from each block. Remove the paper foundation from each block.

Quilt Assembly

1. Arrange the blocks along with the large and small cream triangles according to the diagram below.

2. Sew the blocks into rows, matching seams and corners. Press. Sew the rows together and press.

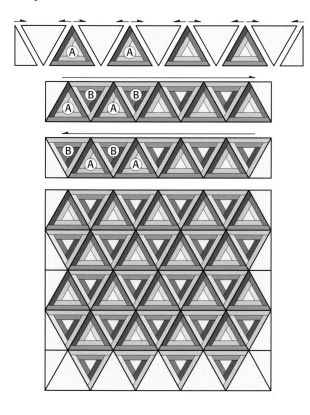

3. Square the corners to prepare for mitered borders. Mark the wrong side of the quilt with a dot ¼" from each corner. (See "Mitered-Corner Borders" on page 22.)

4. Sew the 1½" x 42" dark blue strips together end to end to make one long strip. Repeat with the 1½" x 42" dark purple and dark green strips. You will have one long strip of each of the three different dark colors.

5. Sew the long edges of the strips together as shown to make a strip set. Press toward the dark purple.

Make 1 long strip set.

6. Cut two side borders, 60" long, from the strip set. Cut a top and a bottom border, 46" long, from the strip set.

7. Mark the center of each border strip and the center of each side of the quilt top. Pin the borders to the quilt top, matching the center points. Sew the borders to the quilt, stopping and backstitching at the ¼" mark on each corner of the quilt. Be careful not to catch the border from another side in your seam.

8. Miter the corners, being careful to cut and stitch accurately. Match the seams at the corners. Press.

Finishing

1. Your quilt top is complete, and it's time to sandwich it with backing and batting. (Refer to "Layering" on page 24.) Quilt either by machine or by hand. My quilt is machine quilted with lots of swirls, adding curves and motion to this fun design. Trim excess batting and backing from the edges.

2. Piece the 2½"-wide dark purple strips end to end to make one long binding strip. Fold the strip in half lengthwise, wrong sides together, and press. Sew the raw edges of the binding to the front of your quilt. Fold the binding over to the back and hand stitch. (See "Binding" on page 24.)

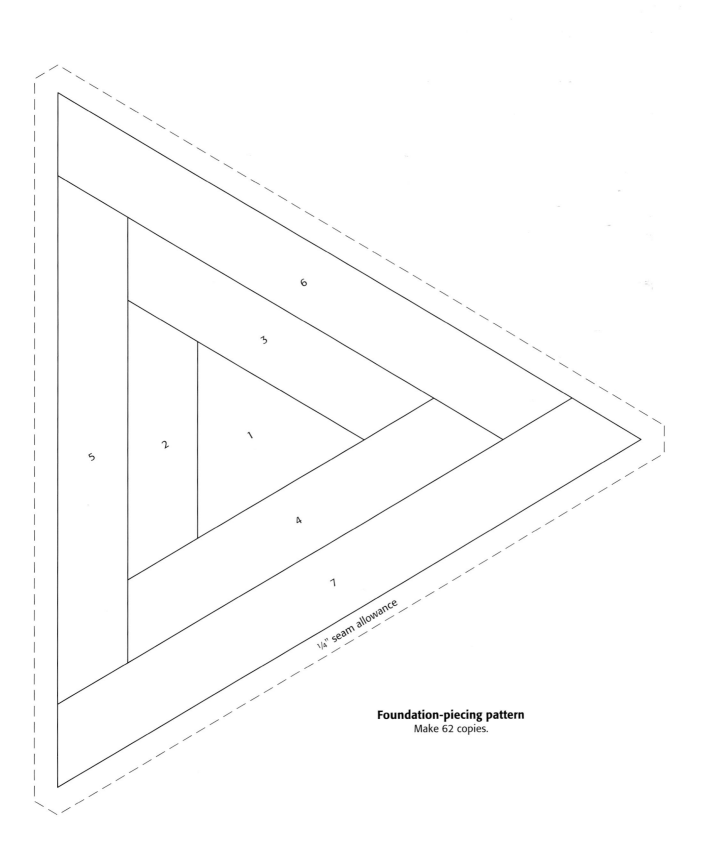

1/4" seam allowance

Foundation-piecing pattern
Make 62 copies.

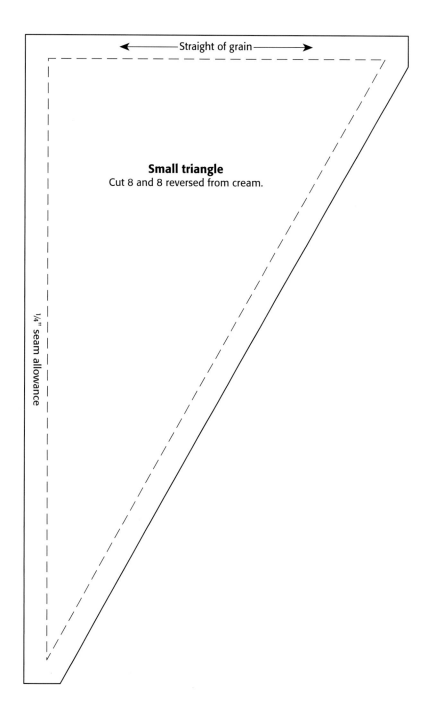

Straight of grain

Small triangle
Cut 8 and 8 reversed from cream.

¼" seam allowance

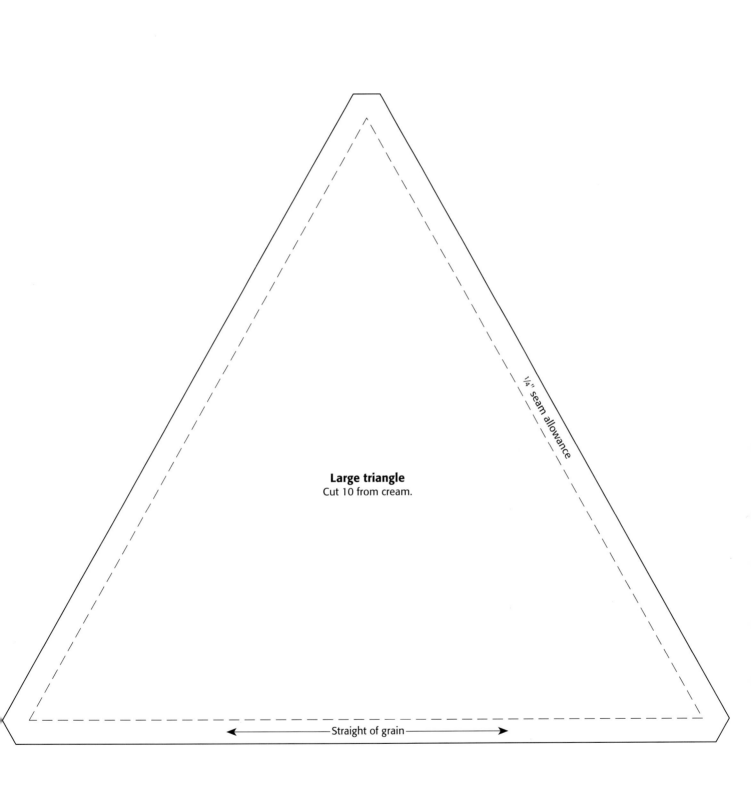

Large triangle
Cut 10 from cream.

¼" seam allowance

Straight of grain

Chapter 9

ABBY SETTLED into her chair next to Mary. Her Log Cabin quilt was bundled into her basket, along with some cinnamon buns she'd baked for the first quilting bee since last fall. Excitement was in the air as the ladies gathered once again after the long, bitter winter. So much news to catch up on!

They gathered at the church because it had the biggest room of any building in town. None of their houses were large enough to host the bee. The ladies chattered pleasantly as they set up the quilt frame.

"Abby, did you bring it?" Mary whispered, her eyes alive with curiosity.

Abby smiled and nodded.

"Well?" Mary laughed. "Let's see it. I can't wait any longer."

Abby lifted a parcel out of her basket. She had wrapped the quilt in a piece of muslin to protect it from dust. Carefully she unfolded the muslin and took out the Log Cabin quilt.

"I'm calling it my Log Cabin quilt. It's the first quilt I made in our new cabin, and the strips remind me of logs!" Abby unfolded the quilt and held up one corner for Mary to see. One by one, the ladies came over to see the new quilt. Other ladies grabbed the remaining corners, and before Abby knew what was happening, the quilt was displayed for all to see.

"I ain't never seen the like!" came a voice.

"My, my! How'd you think to do that?" came another voice.

"Would you lookee there!"

"That is just beautiful!" Several women's voices joined in the praise.

Abby, who never liked to be the center of attention, blushed as the compliments flew. This quilt had been her best friend during the hardest winter she'd ever endured. It had been in her hands while tears fell, when smiles peeked out during daydreams of better days, and it had listened to her talk when there was no one else. She knew every stitch and every piece of fabric. This quilt held an account of Abby's winter, but only Abby knew how to read it.

"Do we get to quilt it?" someone asked.

"I'd be honored to have your stitches in my quilt," Abby said.

"I say we put this one on the frame first. I just want to look at it some more," Mary suggested. Laughter rang out.

"I'm going to make one like this for my own house! Well, I wonder what it would look like if you turned some blocks . . ." the voice trailed off as one lady pondered a new design.

Quickly the muslin was stretched on the frame and the wool laid down. Almost reverently the ladies laid the Log Cabin quilt on top and began to baste.

Soon the basting was done, and the quilting started. The chattering had nearly

stopped as each lady was contemplating her own Log Cabin quilt. Each one studied the block and its construction, thinking about the fabric in her own trunk.

Abby was beaming from all the kindness and compliments bestowed on her quilt by the other women—except for Mrs. Lewis. She had scowled all day. Even Rebecca wasn't sitting next to her mother. What a sour woman, Abby thought to herself. Why was she always scowling? Never a kind word for anyone. Maybe no one ever had a kind word for her, either.

As Abby stitched and listened to the conversation around her, she noticed Rebecca. Gone was the unkempt girl they'd found last month. Rebecca's hair shone, and her cheeks bloomed like roses. Her face was lit up by a smile. Abby looked at her carefully. Why, she's expecting! Abby's heart leaped within her chest. A baby! Surely her mother had noticed, but where was her joy?

Abby bit her lip to keep from laughing out loud. She could hardly wait to tell George they were going to be grandparents.

After the bee, as everyone was packing up their needles and scissors, Abby wandered over to Mrs. Lewis. She placed her hand warmly on her shoulder.

"Mrs. Lewis," Abby smiled directly into her eyes, "I just want to tell you how pleased we are to have Rebecca in our family. She's a lovely woman; you taught her well."

Abby paused for a moment before going outside to find George. Mrs. Lewis stood there, her eyes wide and mouth open. But then the corners of her mouth tilted upwards ever so slightly.

Abby looked back and waved. Mrs. Lewis raised her hand in a small uncertain wave.

"George, you'll never guess! Try and guess!" Abby smiled into his eyes, bouncing a little in excitement.

Lone Star Log Cabin

Made by Karen Murphy, 50½" x 50½"; quilted by Ann Trotter

*I*t is fun to imagine all the different designs the members of Abby's quilting bee might have created. Those patterns would inspire other quilters, who would experiment with more designs, in a continuing legacy all the way to quilters in the twenty-first century. "Lone Star Log Cabin" is a contemporary-looking quilt with strong traditional foundations. A classic Lone Star quilt has eight star points made from diamond-shaped pieces. I created the diamonds with Log Cabin construction and set the blocks so they form concentric rings of color to make this dynamic-looking quilt.

BLOCK NAME: Diamond Log Cabin
FINISHED BLOCK SIZE: 4¾" side of finished
    diamond
SKILL LEVEL: Experienced

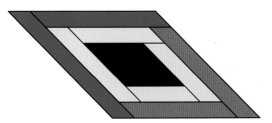

Materials

Yardages are based on 42"-wide fabric.

- ⬦   2⅜ yards of black solid for blocks, borders, and binding
- ⬦   ⅞ yard of dark blue solid for blocks and pieced inner border
- ⬦   ¾ yard of light blue solid for blocks and pieced inner border
- ⬦   ¾ yard of dark pink solid for blocks and pieced inner border
- ⬦   ⅝ yard of light pink solid for blocks and pieced inner border
- ⬦   3⅜ yards of backing
- ⬦   60" x 60" piece of batting (twin)
- ⬦   Freezer paper or template plastic

Cutting

The small diamond pattern is on page 101.

Fabric	First Cut	Second Cut	Location
Black (see below for cutting layout)	1 square, 21¼" x 21¼"	Cut twice diagonally to make 4 large triangles.* ⊠	Side triangles
	6 squares, 4" x 4"	Cut each square twice diagonally to make 24 triangles. ⊠	Pieced border
	4 squares, 3¾" x 3¾"		Border corners
	24 squares, 2¼" x 2¼"	Cut each square once diagonally to make 48 triangles. ◻	Pieced border
	4 squares, 10" x 10"		Corner squares
	6 strips, 2¼" x 42"	48 rectangles, 2¼" x 4½"	Piece 1
	3 strips, 2½" x 42"	48 squares, 2½" x 2½"	Pieced border
	5 strips, 2½" x 42"		Outer border
	6 strips, 2½" x 42"		Binding
Light pink	11 strips, 1¼" x 42"	48 rectangles, 1¼" x 3¾"	Piece 2
		48 rectangles, 1¼" x 4½"	Piece 3
	2 strips, 1⅞" x 42"	20 of the small diamond template	Pieced border
Light blue	12 strips, 1¼" x 42"	48 rectangles, 1¼" x 4½"	Piece 4
		48 rectangles, 1¼" x 5"	Piece 5
	2 strips, 1⅞" x 42"	28 of the small diamond template	Pieced border
Dark pink	13 strips, 1¼" x 42"	48 rectangles, 1¼" x 5"	Piece 6
		48 rectangles, 1¼" x 5¾"	Piece 7
	2 strips, 1⅞" x 42"	28 of the small diamond template	Pieced border
Dark blue	15 strips, 1¼" x 42"	48 rectangles, 1¼" x 5¾"	Piece 8
		48 rectangles, 1¼" x 6½"	Piece 9
	2 strips, 1⅞" x 42"	20 of the small diamond template	Pieced border

*Immediately after making the diagonal cuts, sew a scant ¼" from all bias edges. This will help ensure that your quilt top remains square.

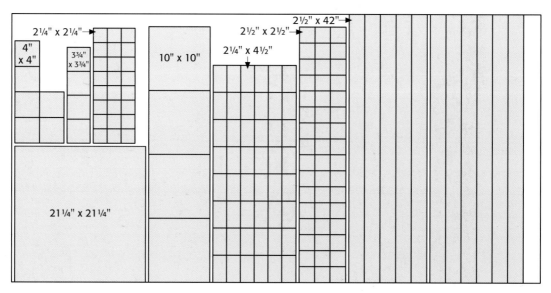

Black fabric cutting layout

Block Construction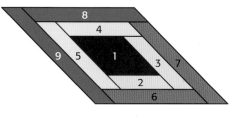

1. Make 48 copies of the foundation-piecing pattern on page 101.

2. Paper piece 48 Diamond Log Cabin blocks, following the fabric placement in the cutting chart and referring to the illustration below. (See "Paper Foundation Piecing" on page 16.)

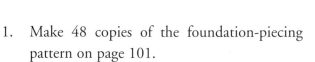

Make 48.

⁓

When sewing the last row of logs, sew all the way to the edge of the fabrics. This way, when you trim the block, the seams will reach clear to the edge.

⁓

3. Trim the excess fabric from each block. On the wrong side of the diamonds, mark a dot ¼" from each corner. Remove the paper foundations. Press all blocks carefully so that they don't stretch out of shape.

Quilt Assembly

1. Matching the corner marks, sew six diamonds together as shown to form one of the points of the star. Repeat to make four units. Press.

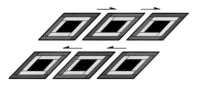

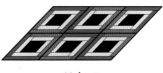

Make 4.

2. Matching the corner marks, sew six diamonds together as shown to make a star point that is a mirror image of the units sewn in step 1. Repeat to make four units. Press.

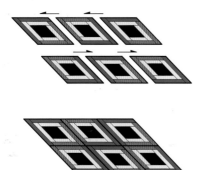

Make 4.

3. Place a star unit from step 1 right sides together with a star unit from step 2. Starting at the tip, stitch the seam, stopping and backstitching at the corner dot. Press the seam to one side. Repeat to make four units.

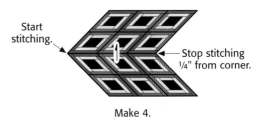

Start stitching.

Stop stitching ¼" from corner.

Make 4.

4. Sew two of the units from step 3 together to form half of the star, stopping and backstitching at the corner dot. Press. Repeat with the remaining two units from step 3. You will have two half-star units.

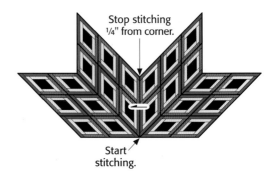

Stop stitching ¼" from corner.

Start stitching.

5. Place the two half-star units right sides together. Start stitching, and backstitch at the corner dots. Match the corner dots of the diamonds as you sew. Stop stitching at the corner dot and backstitch. Press.

Start stitching ¼" from corner.

Stop stitching ¼" from corner.

6. Sew the four black side triangles to the quilt top. (See "Set-in Seams" on page 18.)

7. Again using set-in seams, sew the 10" black squares to the corners of the quilt top. Press.

8. On the wrong side of the small diamonds, place a mark at each corner as indicated by the dots on the template.

9. Arrange four light pink diamonds, one 4" black quarter-square triangle, two 2¼" black half-square triangles, and two 2½" black squares as shown. Sew the light pink diamonds together, stopping and backstitching ¼" from the corners.

Stop stitching
¼" from corners.

10. Sew the two black squares and the black quarter-square triangle to the light pink diamond unit, setting in the seams. Press. Sew the black half-square triangles to the corners of the unit. Press. Repeat with the remaining light pink diamonds to make five border units.

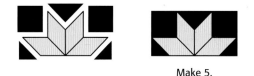

Make 5.

11. Repeat steps 9 and 10 with the dark pink, light blue, and dark blue diamonds. You will have seven dark pink, seven light blue, and five dark blue border units.

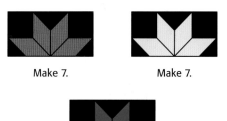

Make 7.   Make 7.

Make 5.

12. Arrange six border units along each quilt edge. You may want to experiment with different arrangements of the colors. Sew the units together, matching the star points, to make four borders. Press.

13. Sew a black 3¾" square to the ends of the top and bottom borders. Press away from the black squares.

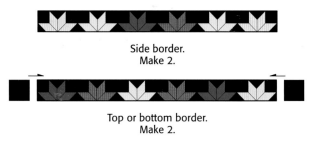

Side border.
Make 2.

Top or bottom border.
Make 2.

14. Sew the pieced side borders to the quilt top. Press toward the borders. Sew the pieced top and bottom borders to the quilt top. Press toward the borders.

I love pieced borders, but it is always a challenge to get them to fit the quilt top. Sometimes you can take slightly larger or smaller seam allowances in the pieced border to make it match the quilt. It is difficult to do that with these borders, however, because the points on the half-star units will not match if you take larger or smaller seams between the border units. If your borders are only slightly larger or smaller than the quilt top (1" or less), ease the excess fabric as you sew the borders to the top. Your machine will do some of the easing for you if you place the piece with the excess fabric against the feed dogs. If your borders are significantly smaller than the quilt top (more than 1"), you can add little strips of black fabric at each end to bring them up to size. If your borders are significantly larger than the top, you can add a thin inner black border to the quilt top. This will change the look of the quilt, giving the Lone Star points the appearance of floating in space instead of touching the borders.

15. Measure the center of the quilt from top to bottom to determine the side outer border measurements. Piece and cut two borders from the 2½" x 42" black strips to this measurement and sew them to the left and right sides of the quilt top. (See "Butted-Corner Borders" on page 21.) Press toward the borders.

16. Measure the center of the quilt from left to right to determine the top and bottom outer border measurements. Piece and cut two

borders from the 2½" x 42" black strips to this measurement and sew them to the top and bottom of the quilt top. Press toward the borders.

Finishing

1. Your quilt top is complete, and it's time to sandwich it with backing and batting. (Refer to "Layering" on page 24.) Quilt either by machine or by hand. My quilt was quilted by machine with in-the-ditch stitching for the diamonds and with curves for the border stars. The black fabric in the background and block centers is densely quilted using a style of quilting made popular by professional machine quilter Karen McTavish. Trim excess batting and backing from the edges.

2. Piece the six remaining 2½" x 42" black strips end to end to make one long binding strip. Fold the strip in half lengthwise, wrong sides together, and press. Sew the raw edges of the binding to the front of your quilt. Fold the binding over to the back and hand stitch. (See "Binding" on page 24.)

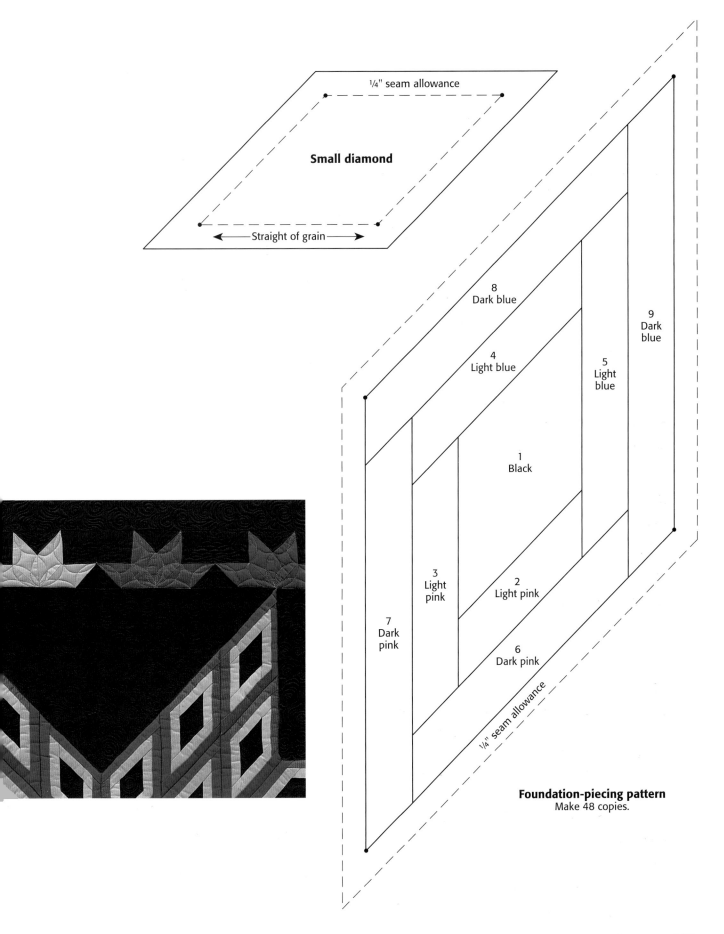

¼" seam allowance

Small diamond

←— Straight of grain —→

8
Dark blue

9
Dark
blue

4
Light blue

5
Light
blue

1
Black

3
Light
pink

2
Light pink

7
Dark
pink

6
Dark pink

¼" seam allowance

Foundation-piecing pattern
Make 48 copies.

Chapter 10

ABBY, I don't know why you had to invite them over for dinner," George grumbled.

"I've already explained it to you! I think they aren't nice to anyone because no one is nice to them. At least I'm trying. And we are related, you know!" Abby set plates on the table.

"I wish you had invited Rebecca and Henry. Then I'd have someone to talk to," George muttered under his breath.

"I heard that!"

George headed out to the barn, kicking a dirt clod. Abby set out platters of sliced bread, made fresh that morning. Ducks were roasting in the oven and green beans were simmering on the stove. A chocolate cake rested on her worktable and coffee bubbled in its pot. Dinner was ready. Where were the Lewises?

"George, you better wash up, dinner's ready!" Abby called out the door.

Abby and George waited for nearly half an hour before they heard horses and a wagon pull up. They looked at each other, shaking their heads.

"Please, come in and sit down." Abby took the bowl of early peas from Mrs. Lewis and set them on the table. "These look delicious!"

"I'm sorry we're late. Wagon wheel broke," Mrs. Lewis said stiffly.

"Oh, that's too bad," George tried to sympathize.

"Dinner's ready. Why don't we all sit down?" Abby indicated their seats and, after they were seated, George said a short blessing.

With an awkward lack of conversation, the dishes were passed around. Mr. Lewis had yet to speak, although he had nodded in George's direction.

"So, isn't it exciting—becoming grandparents?" Abby broke the silence.

"Ain't fittin' to speak of things like that," Mr. Lewis grunted.

"Oh, please excuse me." Abby looked startled.

Mrs. Lewis glanced at her but said nothing.

"How's your crop looking this year, Mr. Lewis?" George attempted.

"Good," he replied between mouthfuls.

The meal seemed to last forever. Finally it was over and Abby brought the cake to the table.

Mrs. Lewis glanced at her husband and then said, "It looks delicious."

"Thank you." Abby sliced the cake and laid the pieces on plates. George passed them to their company first.

"No thanks, don't eat nothin' sweet," Mr. Lewis scowled.

Mrs. Lewis had been about to reach for her plate, but quickly withdrew her hand at

his remark. "Thank you for the meal. Now we got to go."

Mr. and Mrs. Lewis scooted their chairs back and headed for the door.

"Oh wait, your bowl!" Abby called.

"I'll get it later," came the response of Mrs. Lewis from the porch.

Abby and George stared at each other as the Lewises left in their wagon.

"Well, if that don't beat all!" George exclaimed. "I've never had an evening like that in my life!"

"I just don't know what to say! That was . . . strange," Abby finished.

Quietly Abby started washing the dishes and George went out to check the stock.

Later, chores finished, they sat on the porch watching the sunset.

Abby reached for his hand. "George, I wonder what happened to make them so grumpy and irritable?"

He covered her hand with his larger one. "You got me. I'm glad the evening's over though. I never want to spend another one like that again."

"Well, I think I'll invite Mrs. Lewis over next week," Abby mused.

"What?" George was incredulous.

"I think it's her husband that makes her so sour. Didn't you see how he treated her? I'll ask her over alone, and we can plan a baby quilt. A baby always brings family together, and Mr. Lewis can't fault two women for 'speakin' of it.'" She grinned, mimicking his grumpy voice.

George laughed out loud and squeezed her hand. "You do what you want to, but I'll be sure to be gone that day."

And so they sat, enjoying their quiet companionship, watching as the sunset colors ranged from orange to pink, dark purple to lavender.

When darkness fell, George stood and offered Abby his arm. "It's time to go crawl under that Log Cabin quilt of yours." He pulled her close and kissed her warmly. "I love you, Abby."

She nestled her head against his shoulder. "I love you too, George."

Grandmother's Flower Garden

Made by Karen Murphy, 53½" x 59½"; quilted by Ann Trotter

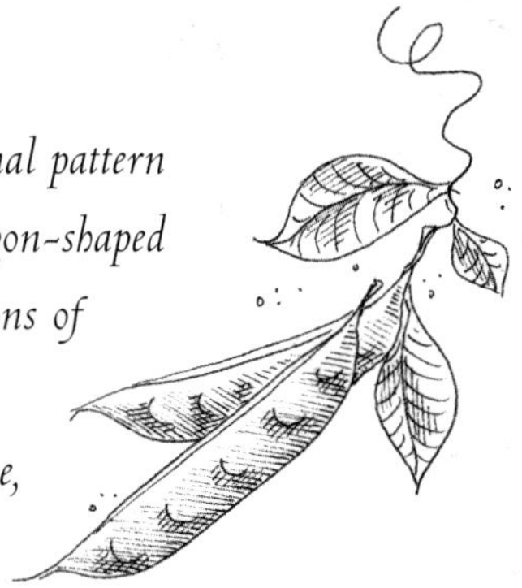

*W*ith Abby and George soon to become grandparents, I found myself considering the traditional pattern called "Grandmother's Flower Garden." In this pattern, the quilt is made entirely of hexagon-shaped pieces of fabric. The colors are usually arranged to form "flowers" consisting of a ring of six hexagons of one color and a center hexagon in a different color. Instead of using a single piece of fabric for each hexagon, I made each with Log Cabin construction and arranged the colors so the quilt looks like one, large flower. Yes, this quilt has set-in seams, but it will go together easier than you think.

BLOCK NAME: Hexagon Log Cabin
FINISHED BLOCK SIZE: 6½" diameter
SKILL LEVEL: Experienced

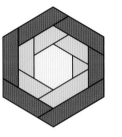
Block A

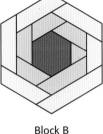
Block B

Materials

Yardages are based on 42"-wide fabric.

✧ 2 yards of light pink solid for blocks and binding
✧ 1½ yards of white solid for border hexagons
✧ 1½ yard of medium pink solid for blocks
✧ 1¼ yards of dark pink solid for blocks
✧ 3½ yards of backing
✧ 62" x 68" piece of batting (twin)
✧ Freezer paper or template plastic

Cutting

The pattern for the border hexagon is on page 110.

Fabric	First Cut	Second Cut	Location
Light pink	2 strips, 3¾" x 42"	21 rectangles, 3¼" x 3¾"	Piece 1 (block A)
	19 strips, 1¾" x 42"	24 rectangles, 1¾" x 3¾"	Piece 8 (block B)
		96 rectangles, 1¾" x 4¾"	Pieces 9, 10, 11, 12 (block B)
		24 rectangles, 1¾" x 6"	Piece 13 (block B)
	8 strips, 2½" x 42"		Binding
Medium pink	27 strips, 1¾" x 42"	45 rectangles, 1¾" x 2½"	Piece 2 (blocks A, B)
		180 rectangles, 1¾" x 3¾"	Pieces 3, 4, 5, 6 (blocks A, B)
		45 rectangles, 1¾" x 4¾"	Piece 7 (blocks A, B)
Dark pink	17 strips, 1¾" x 42"	21 rectangles, 1¾" x 3¾"	Piece 8 (block A)
		84 rectangles, 1¾" x 4¾"	Pieces 9, 10, 11, 12 (block A)
		21 rectangles, 1¾" x 6"	Piece 13 (block A)
	2 strips, 3¾" x 42"	24 rectangles, 3¼" x 3¾"	Piece 1 (block B)
White	32 of the border hexagon templates		Border

Block Construction

1. Make 45 copies of the foundation-piecing pattern on page 109.

2. Make 21 of block A and 24 of block B, following the fabric placement in the cutting chart and referring to the illustrations at right. (See "Paper Foundation Piecing" on page 16.) When piecing the outer round of logs, sew a little past the edge of the paper pattern.

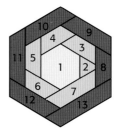

Block A.
Make 21.

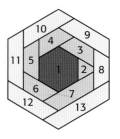

Block B.
Make 24.

3. Trim the excess fabric from each block. On the wrong side of the hexagons, mark a dot ¼" from each corner. Remove the paper foundations. Press all blocks carefully so that they don't stretch out of shape.

Quilt Assembly

1. On the wrong side of the plain white border hexagons, place a mark ¼" from each corner.

2. Arrange the A blocks, B blocks, and white hexagons according to the following diagram.

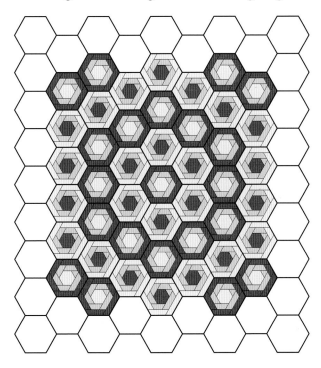

3. Sew the blocks and hexagons together, starting and stopping with backstitches at the ¼" marks. (See "Set-in Seams" on page 18.) I find it easiest to sew the blocks and hexagons into rows and then sew the rows together. You can also start by sewing the center block to the six blocks that surround it, and then continue to work your way outward.

Finishing

1. Your quilt top is complete, and it's time to sandwich it with backing and batting. (Refer to "Layering" on page 24.) Quilt either by machine or by hand. My quilt was quilted by machine, with a rose in the center of each block and trailing leaves filling the border. Trim excess batting and backing from the edges.

2. On the front of the quilt, use a pencil or chalk to lightly mark all the outside angles ¼" from the corners.

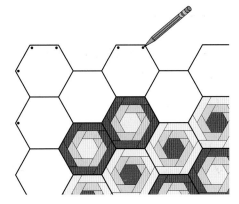

3. Sew the 2½" x 42" light pink strips together end to end to make one long binding strip. Fold the strip in half lengthwise, wrong sides together, and press. (See "Binding" on page 24.)

4. Leave the first 1½" of the binding unsewn and begin sewing the binding about ¾" before a corner on one of the hexagons.

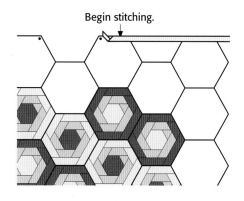

Begin stitching.

5. The outside angles will be sewn just like a regular 90° corner. Stop sewing ¼" from the edge. Backstitch. Remove the quilt from the machine and cut the thread. Fold the binding up and then back down, line up the edges, and continue sewing.

6. On the inside angles, don't stop sewing. Leave your needle down, lift up the presser foot, and pivot the quilt, lining up the binding with the next unsewn quilt edge. Continue sewing.

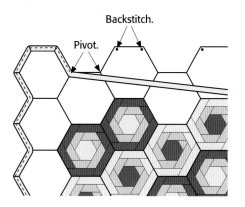

Backstitch.
Pivot.

7. Continue in this manner until you reach the beginning of the binding. Stop sewing after you turn the final corner. Remove the quilt from the machine, trim the end of the binding at a 45° angle, and tuck it into the beginning of the binding strip. Sew the last little bit down, and you are almost done!

8. Fold the binding to the back of the quilt and hand stitch.

☙

I confess, a little wrinkle at an inside corner doesn't bother me, but it may bother some of you! If it does, make a tiny snip in the binding's seam allowance just at the inner points to help the binding lie flat at the corner. You can also tuck and stitch a tiny miter at each inside corner.

☙

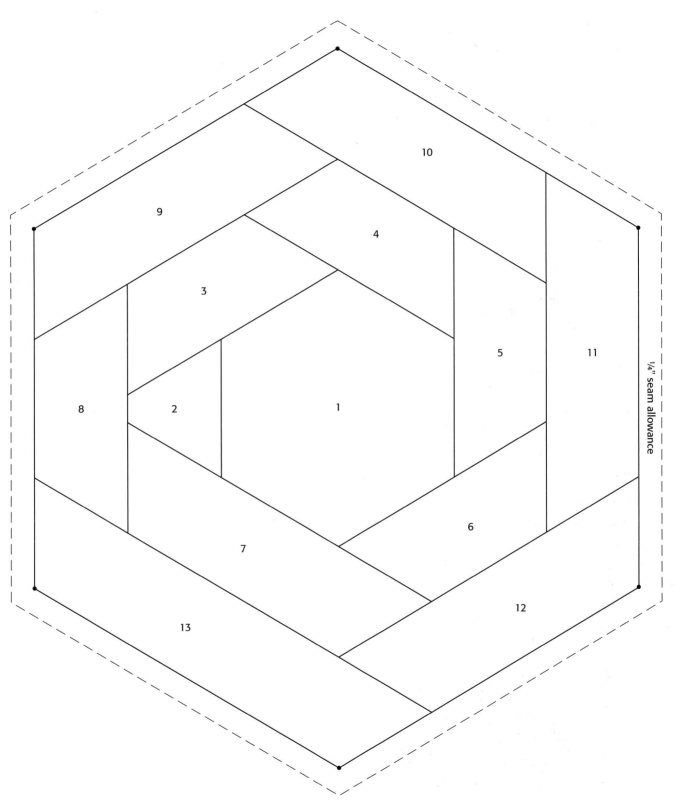

1/4" seam allowance

Foundation-piecing pattern
Make 45 copies.

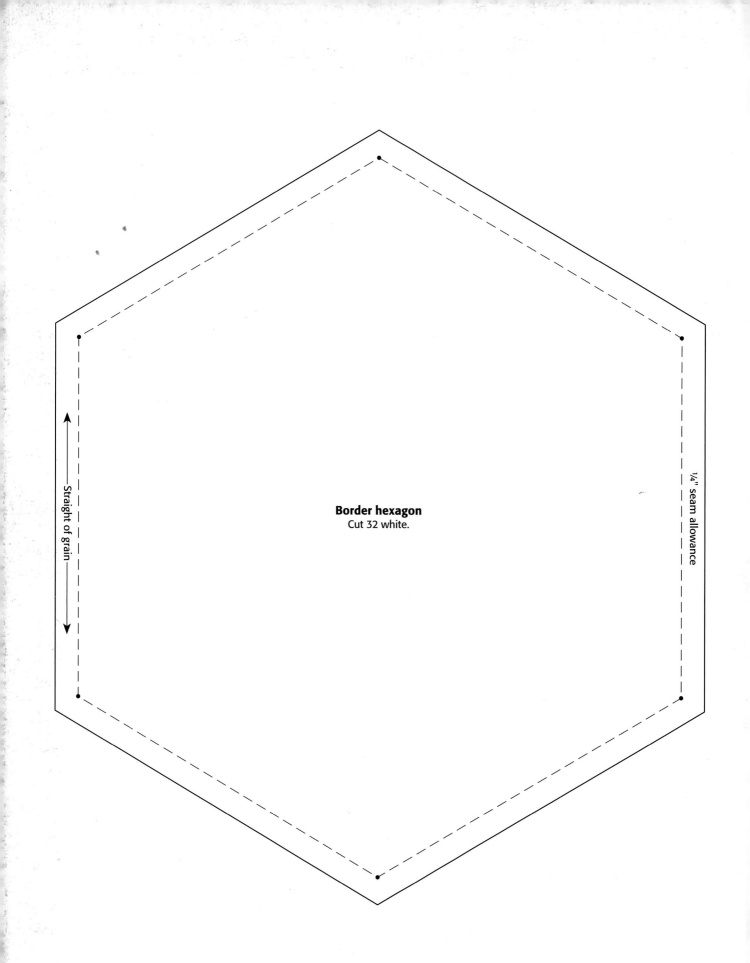

Border hexagon
Cut 32 white.

Straight of grain

¼" seam allowance

∽Acknowledgments∾

ABBY AND GEORGE's story is illustrated by Kris Lammers. (Kris is the author's sister, and the two spent many hours talking over the story and deciding which aspects to illustrate.) So many pictures could have been drawn, but Karen and Kris feel that these are the best of the best. Kris is a self-taught artist with natural talent. She is a freelance illustrator and is busy with a new granddaughter.

Thank you to RJR Fabrics, Moda Fabrics, and Marcus Brothers Textiles Incorporated for supplying beautiful fabrics for the quilts. Heartfelt thanks to Wayne and Gayle Laufer for allowing us to photograph at their lovely log cabin home and to Rosemary and Clifford Bailey of Snohomish, Washington, for the use of their wonderful gardens.

∾ About the Author ∾

MY MOTHER taught me to sew when I was nine years old. I was instantly head over heels in love with the sewing machine and fabric. I made all my own clothes, even prom dresses. I married a military man and we lived in several different states, even spending a few years in Europe. Cultural influences, combined with a love of history, determined many of my design ideas. I made clothing for my children until they were old enough to want "clothes from the mall," and that is when my textile interest changed from garment construction to quilting. I saw a quilted Lone Star wall hanging with appliqué in the setting blocks, and I was entranced! So I taught myself to quilt, at first using garment-construction "rules" until I quickly found out that quilting has different rules! Through much trial and error, I sewed and ripped and sewed my way to a Log Cabin wall hanging. That first project took me more than a year to complete, but every year I improved my technique and my speed. I sold many quilts at craft shows and fairs. After a few years of selling, I realized I wanted more control over the design of my quilts and began my own pattern company, Idaho Quilt Company.